extreme
MINIMALISM
Architecture

Chris van Uffelen

extreme
MINIMALISM
Architecture

DEAR HELEN

ALWAYS KEEP IT SIMPLE

XO

Andy

BRAUN

CONTENTS

PREFACE

In architecture, the term Minimalism refers to an attitude towards purification that encompasses a number of styles. This attitude is of extreme importance in classical modernity. Bauhaus and other Avant-Garde trends of the 1920s and 1930s in particular tried to distance themselves from other styles by their dismissal of decorative elements. Although, even at that time this attitude was far from new. Not only the tendencies that inspired those styles – for example the Reform Classicism of Heinrich Tessenov, or the exposed brick walls of Hendrik Petrus Berlage – appeared in the decoration of a minimalistic building. Earlier inspirations can also be seen, such as the rural classicism style "around 1800" or the so-called Revolutionary Architecture. With the latter – Claude-Nicolas Ledoux, Étienne-Louis Boullée – typical characteristics of Minimalism were already evident, for example the tendency towards large abstract

shapes in the building composition. That these don't always involve the basic geometric forms is made clear by minimalistic, or even completely plain, vaults from the Late Gothic era. The folded vaults of Albrechtsburg in Meissen also belong to Minimalism – despite their complex shape.

This is a good example of what it is that defines Minimalism: not simply the omission of all aesthetic considerations, but rather the concentration on a key idea, which is then consequently carried out. This difference can also already be seen in medieval architecture: while the urban churches belonging to the Mendicant orders omitted a lot of typical Gothic elements, the consequential implementation of aesthetic reduction continued even into the smallest details that can be seen in the Cistercian

Ludwig Mies van der Rohe | Barcelona Pavilion, Barcelona, Spain | 1929
Cellular Vaults | Albrechtsburg Castle, Meissen, Germany | end of 15th century
Étienne-Louis Boullée | Project for the Opéra de Paris | 1781

churches is missing. Urban churches belonging to the Mendicant order are boring, whereas the Minimalism of the Cistercian churches is impressive.

These also show that architectonic Minimalism is not a question of size but rather of attitude, although Cistercian churches in the countryside are significantly larger than their city counterparts. In contrast, small or micro architecture can be entirely non-minimalistic, just think of Baroque chapels or villas in the Historicism style. Even Functionalism is not the same, this is an architecture that meets primary needs, developed in the 1930s, although in the 1950s this type of architecture was often inspired by the works of Mies van der Rohe. The variety of materials used by van der Rohe – for example, the Barcelona pavilion with its travertine, serpentinit, onyx marble, and tinos verde antico, in addition to the glass and steel that characterized Post-war Functionalism – inspired a very modern and extremely luxurious, but nevertheless minimalistic, extreme minimalism.

This volume presents buildings that are set apart by their systematically reduced architectural language, with a design concept based on just a few ideas that are systematically implemented right down to the details. This doesn't mean simply omitting details, but rather the creation of an individual expression that concentrated on just a few materials and which are relatively easy to realize. However, this reduction creates an impressive result. Tadao Ando and Richard Meier are the contemporary masters of such extreme minimalism and both appear in this volume. Lots of younger and less well-known architects also offer excellent building designs. In general, the attitude of the architects if not reduced to the dogmatic "Less is more" promoted by Mies van der Rohe, but rather equates a happy and inspired "Less is all you need".

MINI MODERN MA

MINDFUL

MODEST

NIFOLD

MAGNIFICENT

Squish Studio is located just outside the small town of Tilting, at the eastern end of Fogo Island. The white angular form of the studio reflects the jagged, sharp forms of the rocks upon which it is perched. The compact, trapezium shaped plan is augmented by the extension of the east and west exterior walls to create a sheltered, triangulated south entry deck and a north terrace that overlooks the ocean. From a distant view, the streamlined form of the Squish Studio becomes apparent with its high back and low front designed, in part, to deflect the winds from the stormy North Atlantic. The vertical white planks that line the interior walls are interrupted by a playful series of narrow windows integrated with an expanse of built in cabinetry.

SQUISH STUDIO

A tribute to the landscape... Like a white cliff hanging over the ocean, the studio responds to its surroundings by being at one with the rough and rocky coast of the North Atlantic.

Architects | Saunders Architecture
Project address | Fogo Island, Newfoundland, Canada
Gross floor area | 130 m²
Main materials | wood
Completion | 2011

South-West Elevation 1:100

East Elevation 1:100

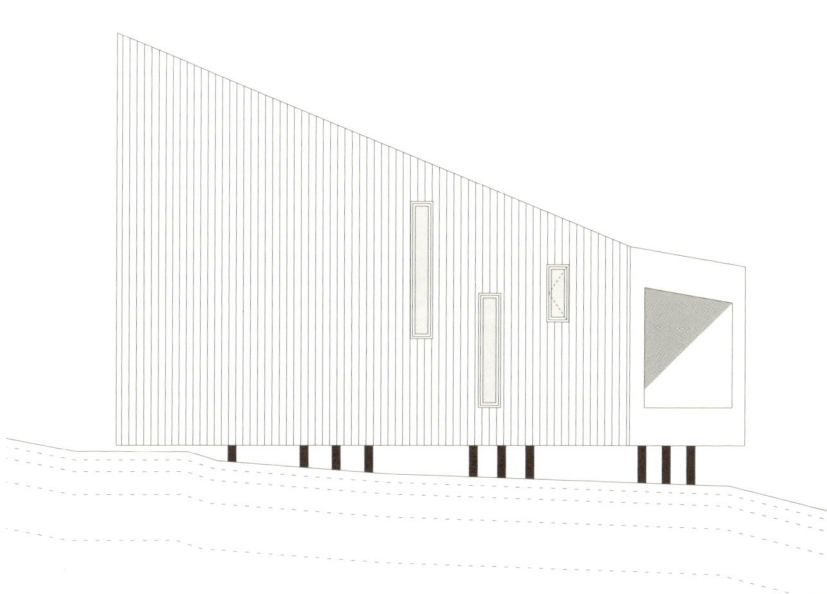

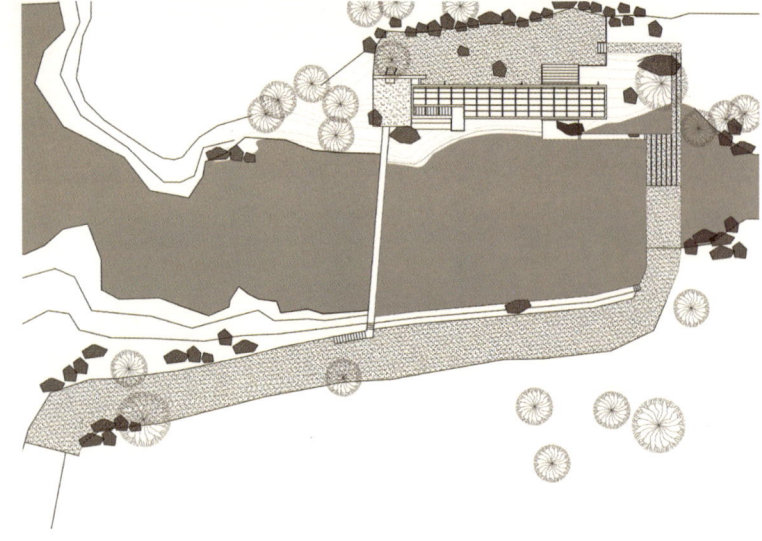

This project is a modest addition to the small village of Huairou on the outskirts of Beijing. On the one hand it adds a modern programmatic element to the village, on the other hand the architects wanted to use architecture to enhance the appreciation of the natural landscape qualities. The delicate choice of materials and the careful positioning allow the building to blend into the landscape. The house frames views towards the surrounding landscape and acts as an embracing shelter. The building is fully glazed to allow for a fully daylit space as well as a response to climatic conditions. The façade tempers the bright light and spreads it evenly throughout the space to provide a perfect reading ambience.

16

LIYUAN LIBRARY

A wooden tree house appears in the middle of the forest. A library designed for both nature lovers and reading enthusiasts. Pure Zen.

Architects | Li Xiaodong Atelier
Project address | Jiaojiehe Village, 100075 Beijing, China
Gross floor area | 175 m²
Main materials | wood, steel
Completion | 2011

Originally opened in 2000, the Autostadt in Wolfsburg has now received a new structure, the Porsche Pavilion. The organically shaped building is located along the central axis of the theme park and offers 400 square meters of exhibition and presentation space. Curving lines and exciting bends make the pavilion a dynamic yet reduced sculpture with its characteristics derived from the Porsche brand image. Its lines pick up speed and slow down just to plunge forward in large curves with ever-changing radii. A matte-finished stainless steel cladding forms the flush envelope of this vibrant structure, creating a continuously changing appearance depending on light and weather conditions. Architecture and landscape, interior and exterior as well as roof and façade are brought together by the architectural concept. The external area around the pavilion was designed by landscape architects WES and integrated into the overall concept of the theme park.

PORSCHE PAVILION

Movement and rapidity: a minimalist steel wave to remember us what Porsche really is about.

Architects | Henn
Project address | Autostadt, Wolfsburg, Germany
Gross floor area | 1,400 m²
Main materials | stainless steel
Completion | 2012

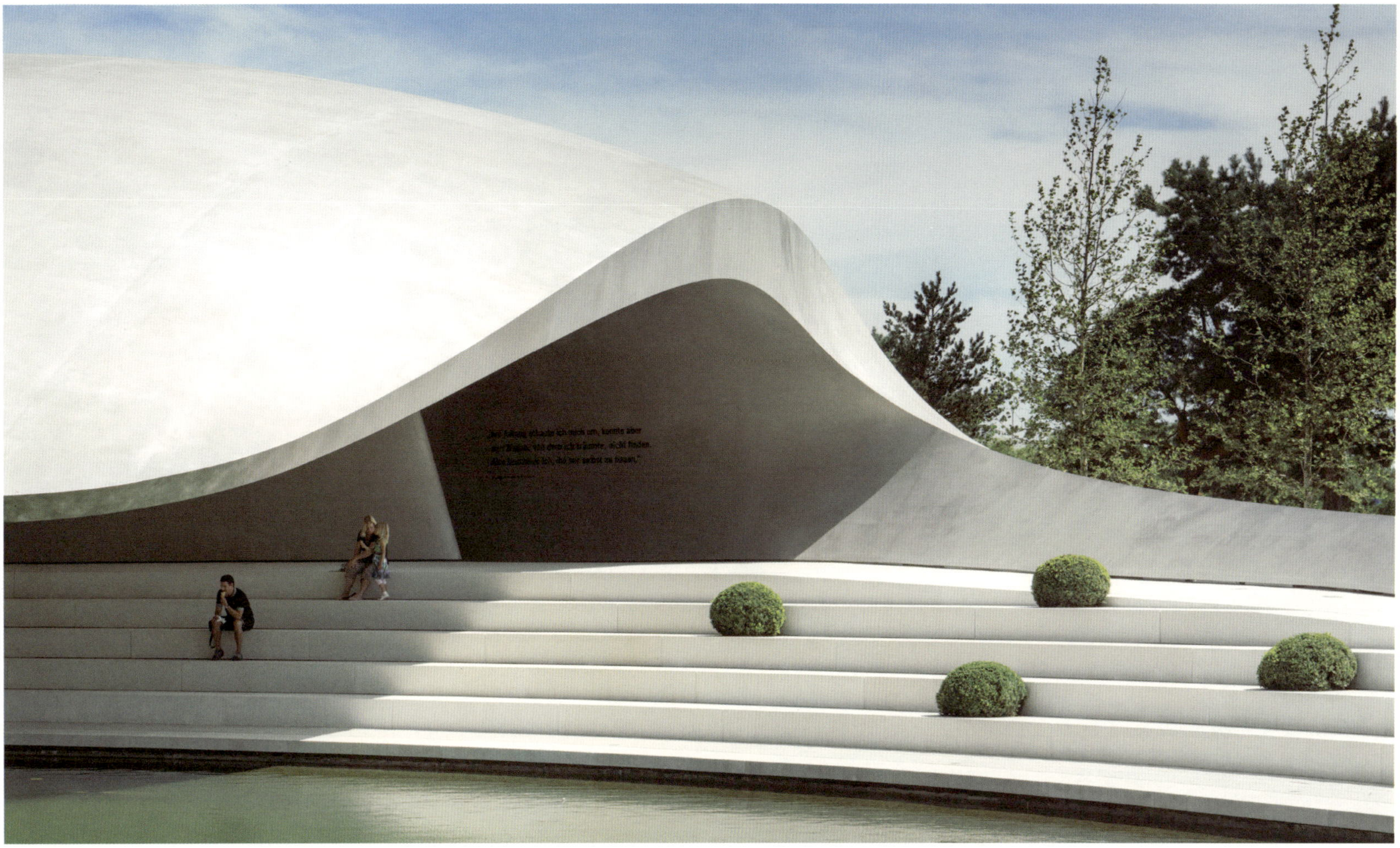

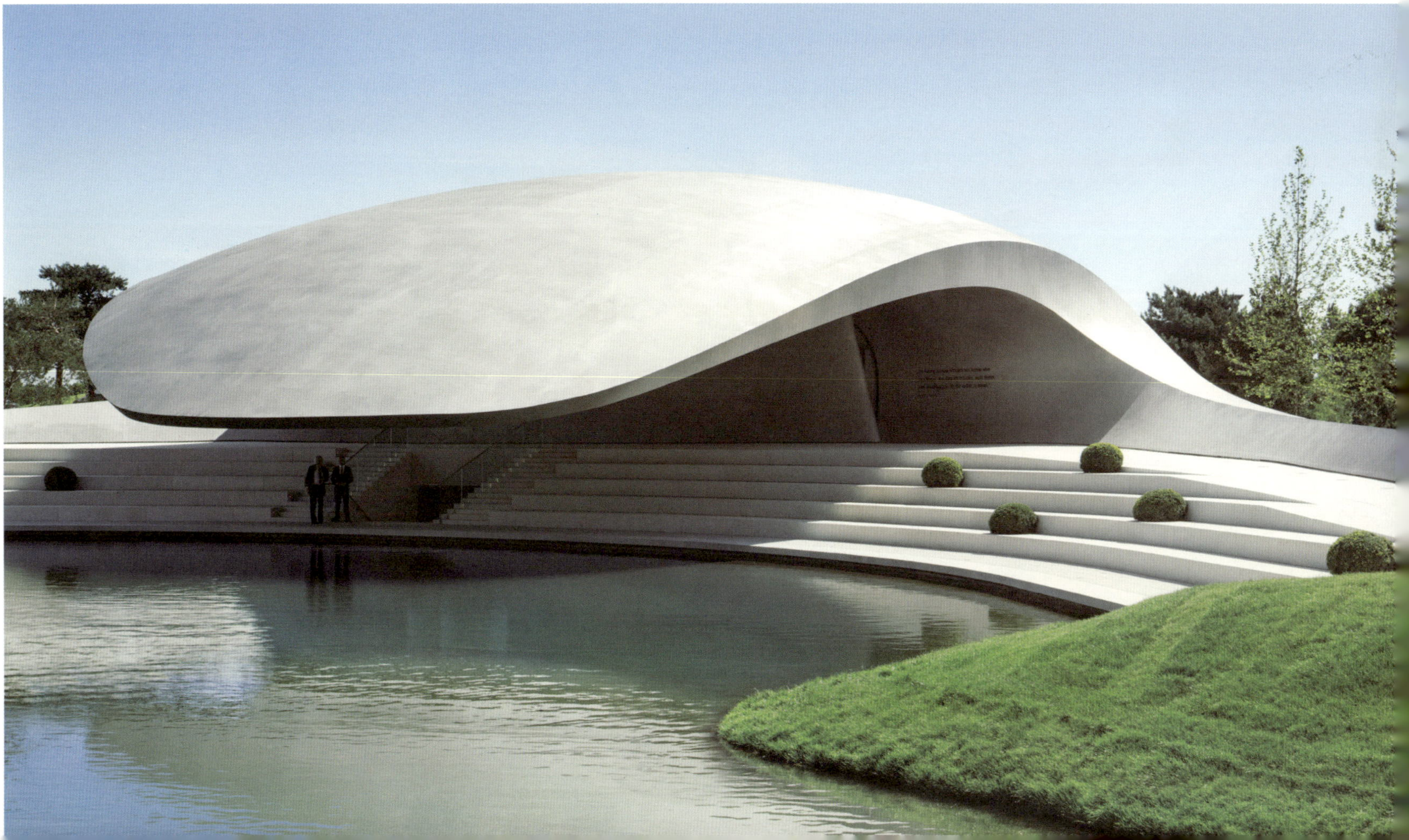

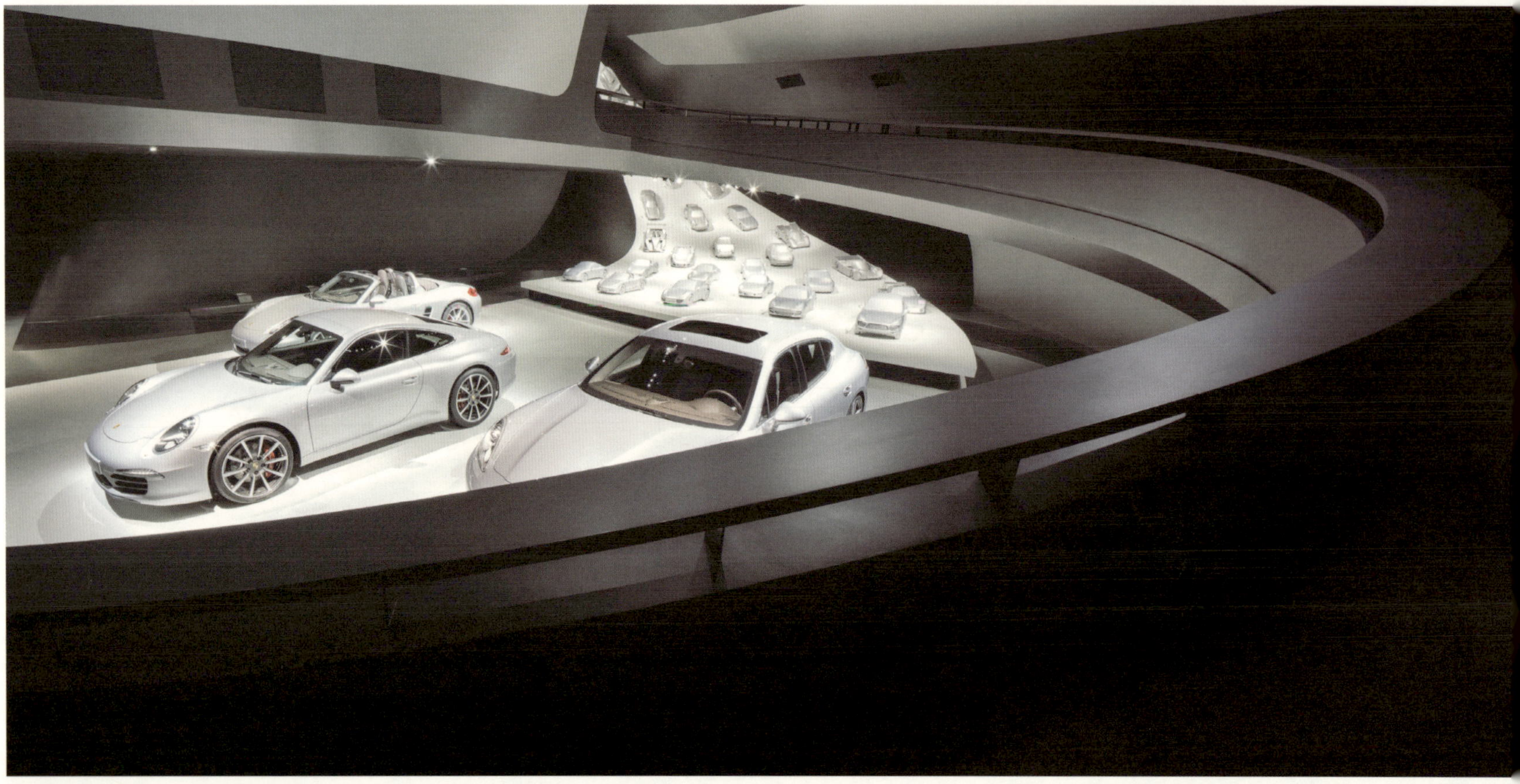

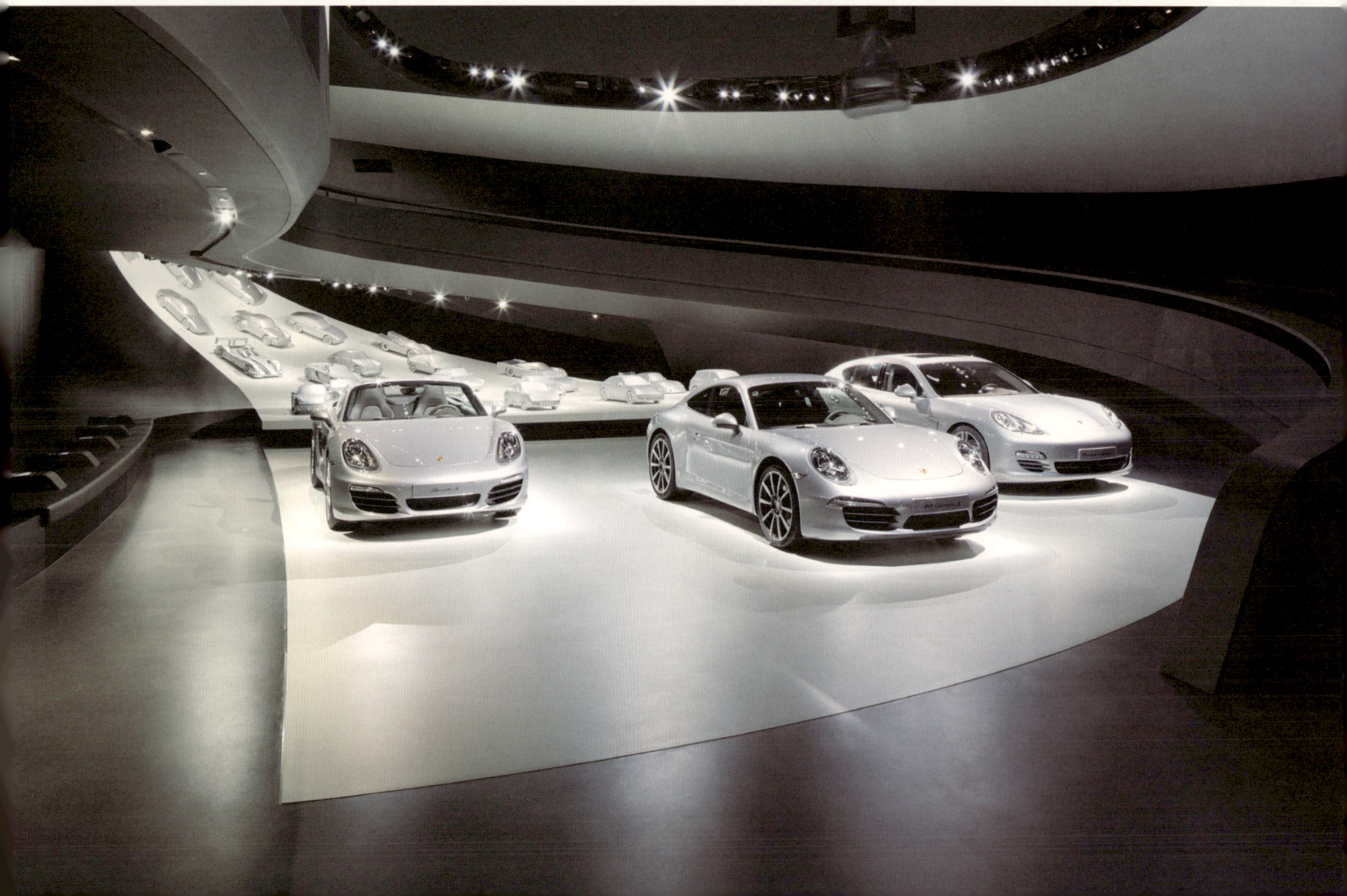

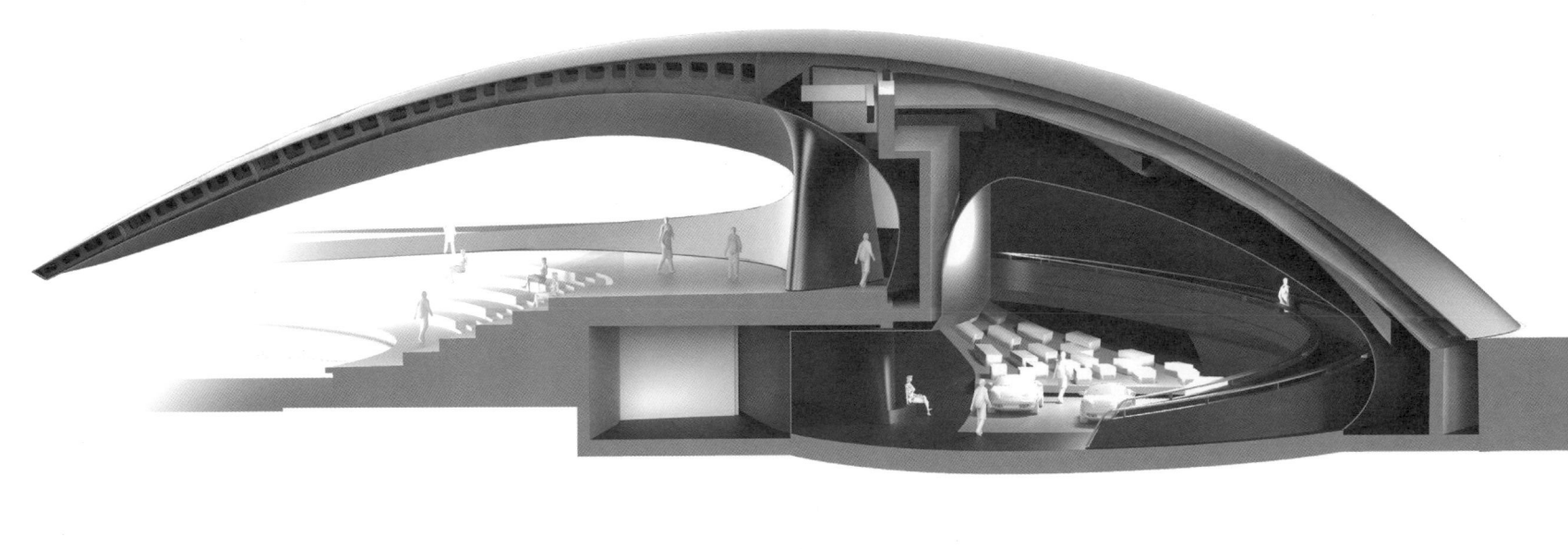

City Green Court is the third of a cluster of buildings in Prague designed by Richard Meier & Partners. Conceived as a geometric volume, it is smaller in scale than its predecessor the City Tower, but equally inspired by the language of Czech Cubism. Its façade incorporates forms reminiscent of this avant-garde movement. The eight-story building is organized around a central daylit atrium surrounded by ultra efficient office space. Inside, the atrium houses a tree and green wall, with bridges above spanning from one side of the space to the other. City Green Court is expected to achieve LEED Platinum certification in the Czech Republic by drastically reducing energy consumption.

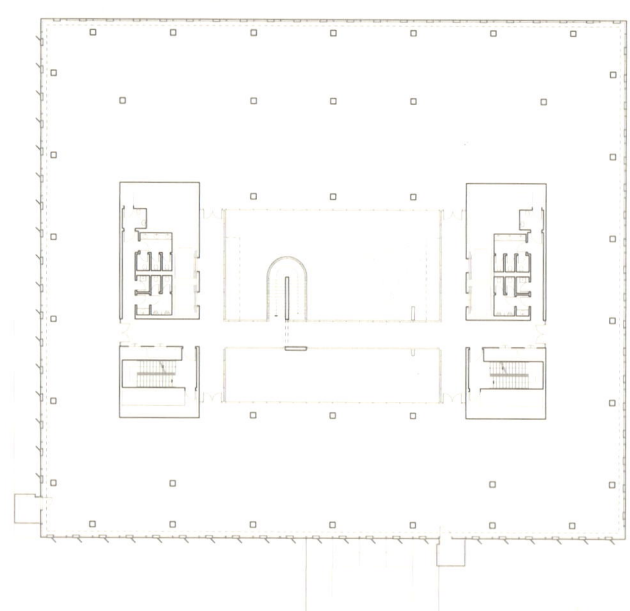

CITY GREEN COURT

Prague's latest architectural exploit: A marvelous
fusion of sustainability and Czech Cubism.

Architects | Richard Meier & Partners Architects
Project address | Hvězdova 1734/2, 140 00 Prague 4, Czech Republic
Gross floor area | 16,300 m²
Main materials | aluminum panels, glass, wood, stone
Completion | 2012

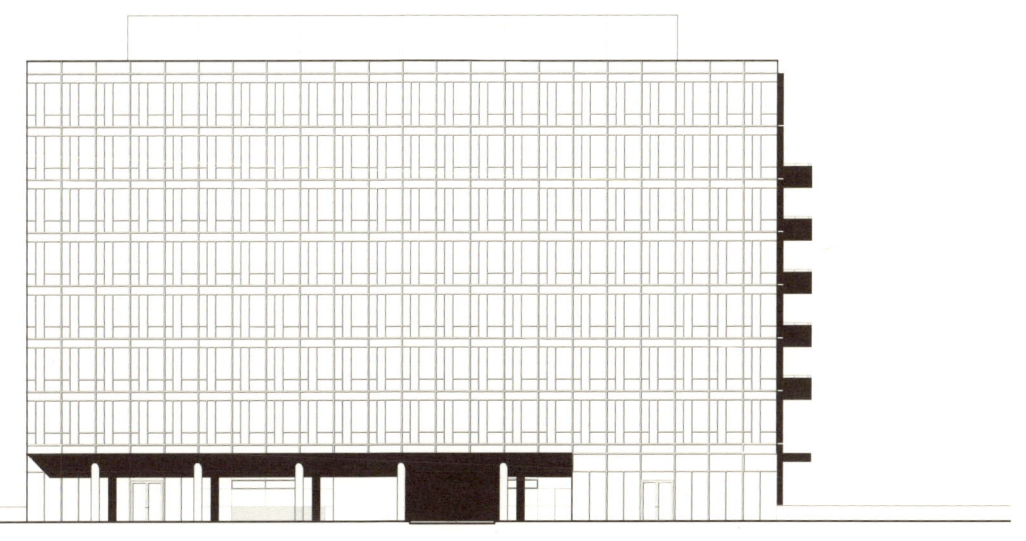

OUTDOOR FOOD COURT

An interplay of indoor and outdoor, of nature and man. All woven together like the branches of the nearby trees.

Architects | jaf:: architecture + design
Project address | Centenario Town, Durazno, Uruguay
Gross floor area | 99 m²
Main materials | stone, concrete
Completion | 2012

This strikingly minimalistic design is a simple, semi-open space that hosts social events and also functions as a food court with barbeque, kitchen, bar and rest rooms. The architectural language shares a dialogue with the existing elements on site and with nature, offering a place to enjoy the outdoors whilst remaining sheltered from the wind and rain and protected from the sun's glare. The walls of natural stone almost look as if they have grown out of the earth, while the flat roof reduces the impact of the building on the views of the surrounding landscape.

33

PINC – Pole for the Creative Industries of Park of Science and Technology, University of Porto – is a recognized center for the creation and production of events. The project evolved from the need to create a meeting point, bringing together employees, customers, and partners. The space needed to be open and flexible, able to serve as a dining area, but also able to accommodate relaxation or discussion, meeting and training. This PINC Pavilion is located in what was formerly a forgotten centennial garden. The pavilion has an open and permeable structure, framed by existing trees. A structure inspired by the images of the timeless ruins. Inside the pavilion warm colors of wood-based panels and the red doors create a welcoming environment.

PINC PAVILION

A modern agora. Inspired by archaeological ruins,
the PINC Pavilion a meeting place for employees,
customers and partners.

Architects | Clínica de Arquitectura
Project address | Praça Coronel Pacheco, n°2, 4050-453, Porto, Portugal
Gross floor area | 70 m²
Main materials | oriented strand board, concrete
Completion | 2012

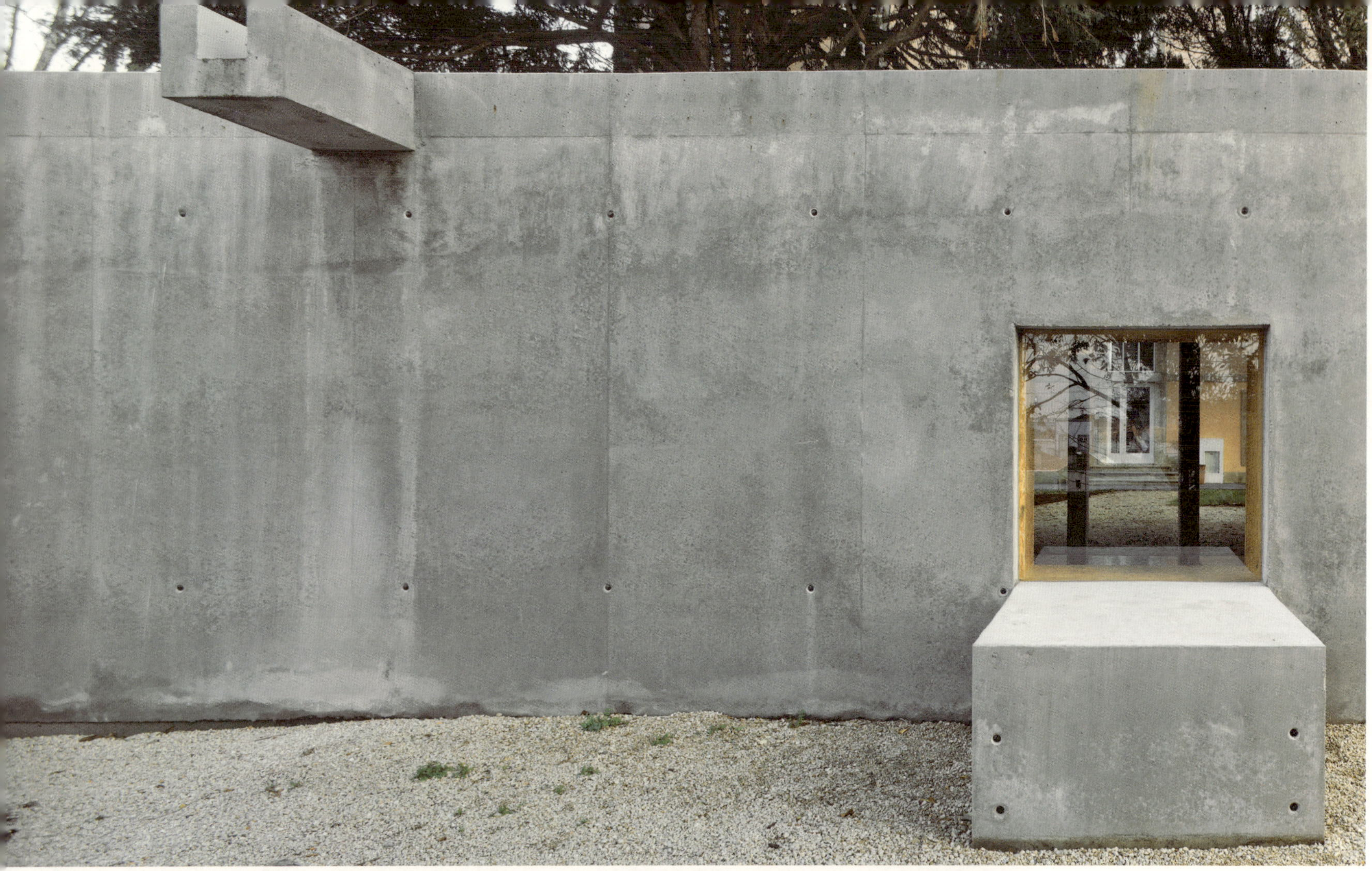

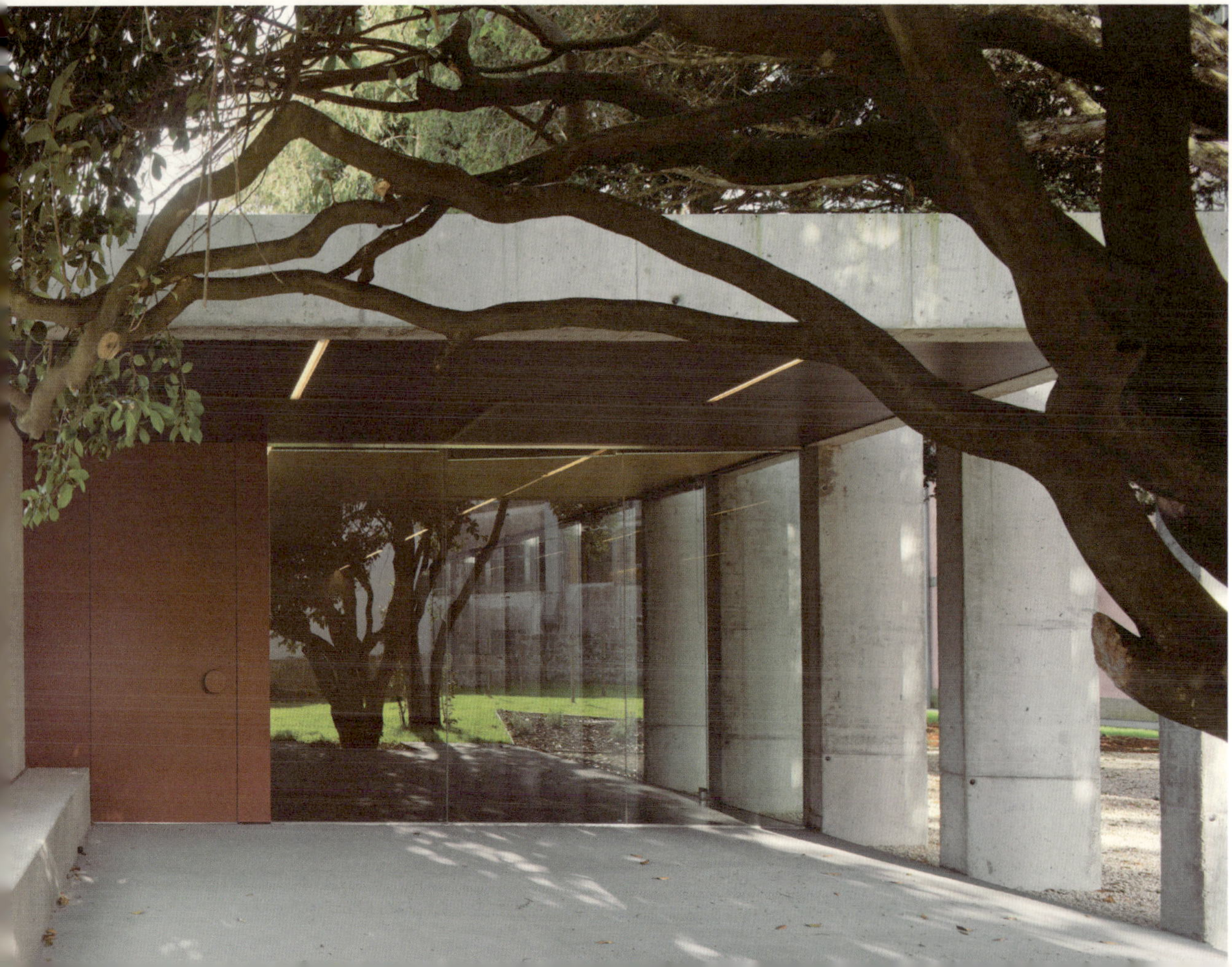

This five-story administration building belonging to Rostock Navy, and the one-story auditorium, have been designed as simple saddle-roofed buildings and are arranged parallel to each other. Their linear volumes suit the urban character of the Hanseatic barracks without establishing an obvious hierarchy. The offices are organized into two groups along either side of a central corridor. The auditorium is connected to the service building by a cross-shaped foyer. Inside the auditorium, the saddle-roofed shape is repeated in an abstract form. This design allows the layered ceiling to incorporate the technical infrastructure, making it almost entirely invisible. The façade structuring follows a strict pattern and has a horizontal orientation.

ADMINISTRATION BUILDING
WITH AUDITORIUM

The archetypical saddle-roofed building and
an example of simple elegance.

Architects | Architekten BKSP Grabau Leiber Obermann und Partner
Project address | Kopernikusstraße 1, 18057 Rostock, Germany
Gross floor area | 6,537 m²
Main materials | concrete
Completion | 2010

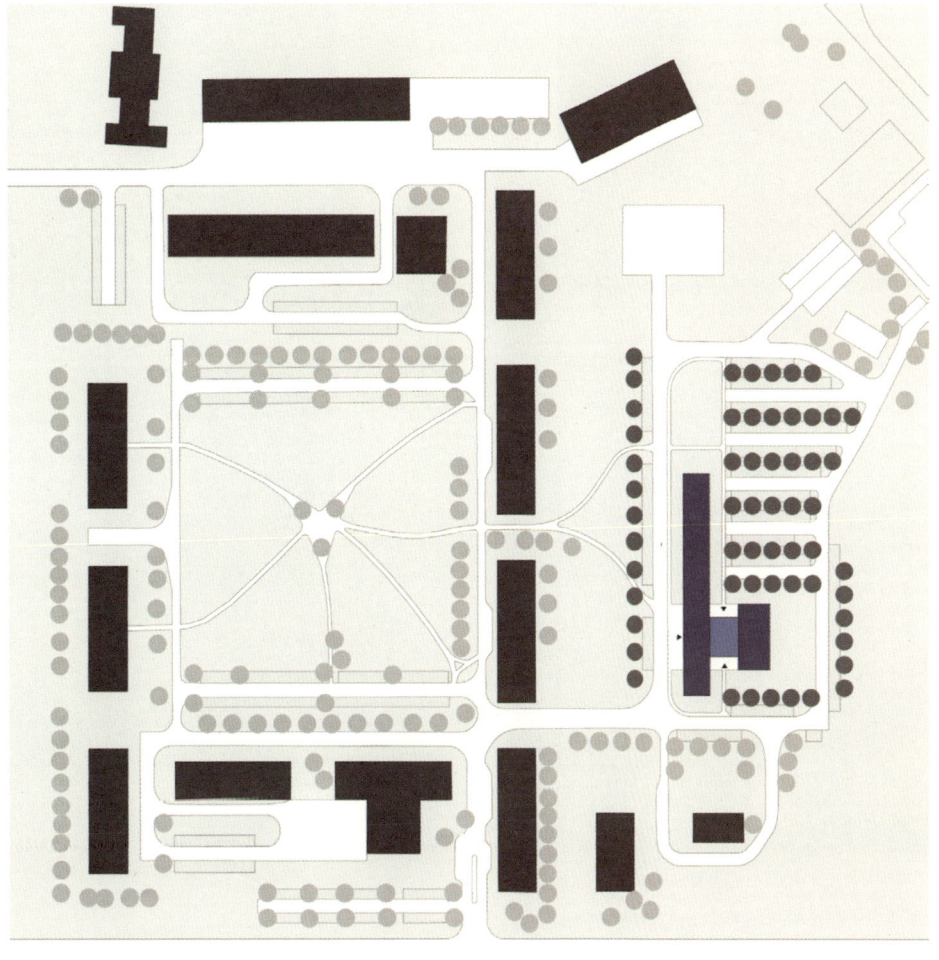

44

EXTENSION WORLD TRADE ORGANIZATION (WTO)

What a clear-cut message! With this new extension, the World Trade Organization shows pure transparency.

Architects | Wittfoht Architekten
Project address | Rue de Lausanne 54, 1211 Geneva, Switzerland
Gross floor area | 14,500 m²
Main materials | glass
Completion | 2012

This new building was designed to complement and realign the urban location. Located between city and lake, the design responds to the existing building. The building is divided into a building base, which houses the communal facilities, and the crystalline volume above, which houses the administration areas. The constructive and clear development of the building creates a high level of transparency and permeability. The volume has a lightweight appearance and a friendly and modern character. The clever organization of the different surfaces retains open spaces, which serve as a place to meet and exchange ideas. The individual levels offer various possibilities for the organization of office space. The office levels features a glazed double curtain façade, which protects against the strong wind and noise. The energy and ventilation concept meets Minergie P standards.

This master plan for the regeneration of Marseille's Vieux Port reclaims the quaysides as a civic space, creating a safe, pedestrian friendly public realm and creating informal venues for performances and events. In order to enlarge the space for pedestrians, the technical installations and boathouses on the quaysides have been replaced with new platforms and clubhouses. Architecturally, the waterfront has been enhanced using very discreet means. At Quai de la Fraternité, the broad eastern edge of the harbor, a blade of reflective stainless steel shelters a flexible new pavilion for events and markets. Open on all sides, the ombrière is held aloft on slender pillars, six meters high. To ensure that the canopy would be sufficiently rigid not to flex and dip under its own weight, it is supported by a stiff central frame and has a gently curving profile, which tapers towards the edges.

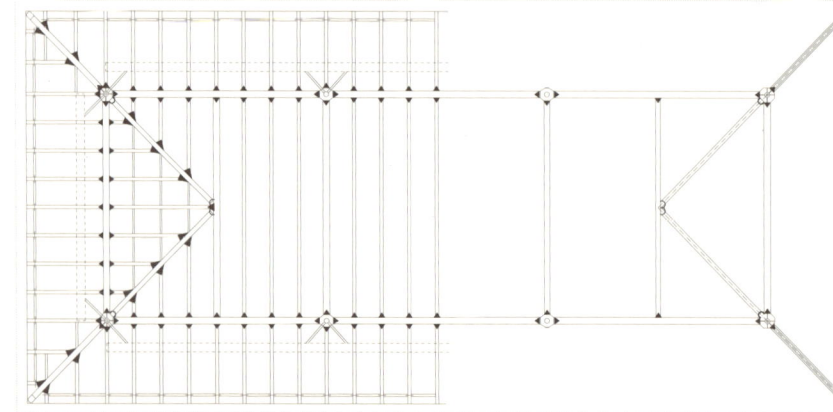

MARSEILLE VIEUX PORT

Southern France upside down. Cool British
style in the Mediterranean.

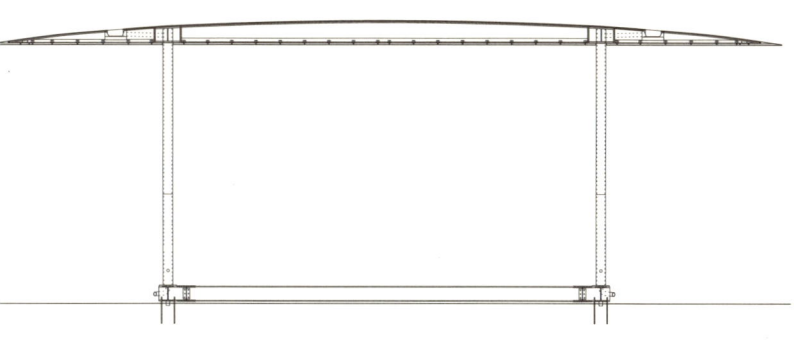

Architects | Foster + Partners
Project address | Vieux Port, Marseille, France
Gross floor area | 46 x 22 m
Main materials | stainless steel
Completion | 2013

49

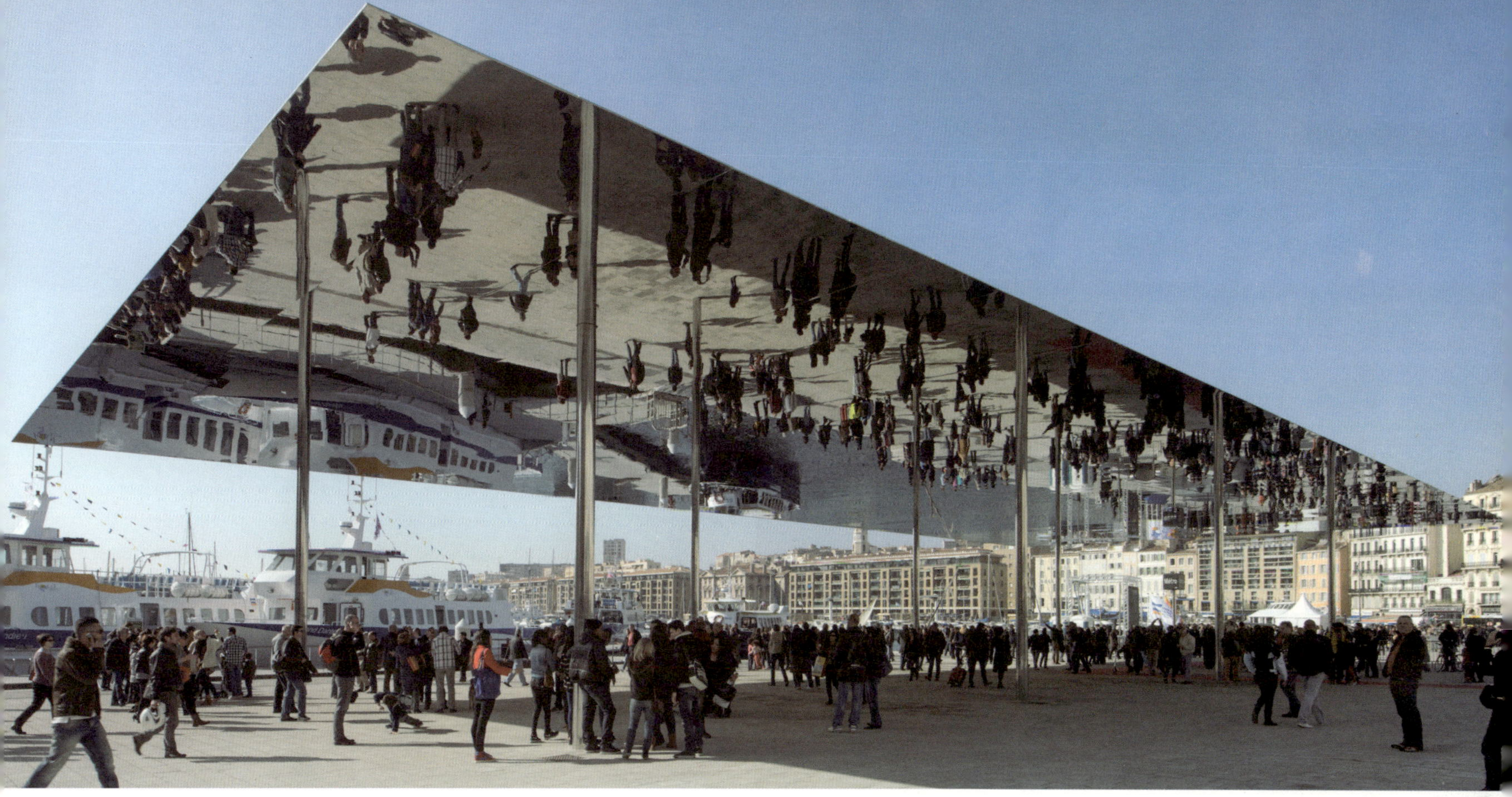

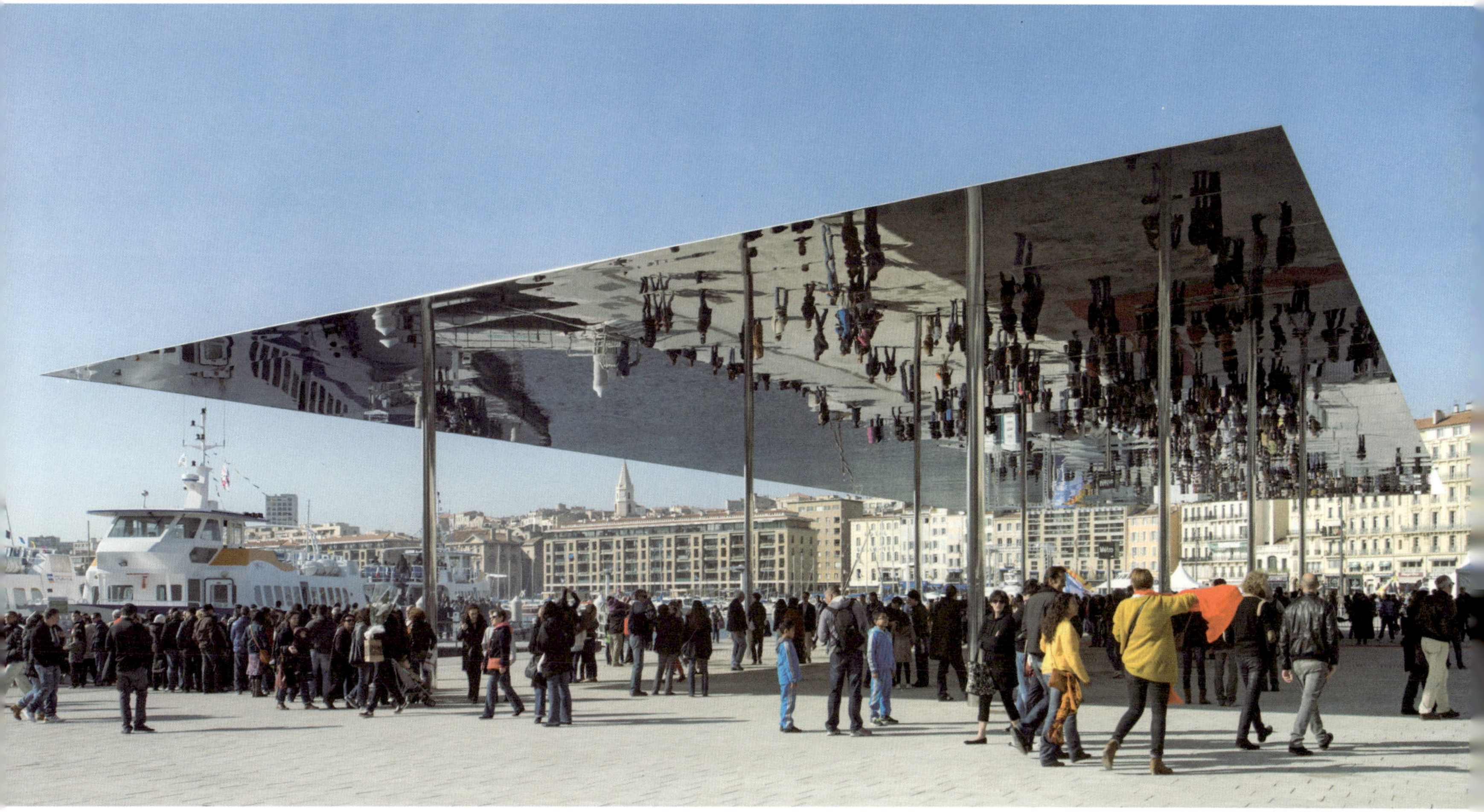

Architects | Amas4arquitectura
Project address | Travesía de la Virgen de Gracia nº2, 49800 Toro, Zamora, Spain
Gross floor area | 771 m²
Main materials | concrete, polycarbonate, glass
Completion | 2010

Located on a steep and elongated site facing a public park, this project involved the construction of a building for a foundation, and an open sports court. The architects established a semi-buried building base that evens the ground and organizes the various entrances to the building. The building seems to almost dematerialize into a deep façade split into different planes. A series of terraces and spaces function as filters and give the south façade its special character. Large terraces with cantilevers help to shade the building and frame views of the landscape. The supporting structure of highly textured concrete is designed to highlight these spatial and perceptive characteristics. The building is encased in a blue and white polycarbonate skin, capable of filtering the natural light that illuminates the interior spaces.

INTRAS CENTER FOR THE MENTALLY DISABLED

Alternating between solid concrete, wells of light and large spaces to breath, the INTRAS develops a secure environment without being oppressive.

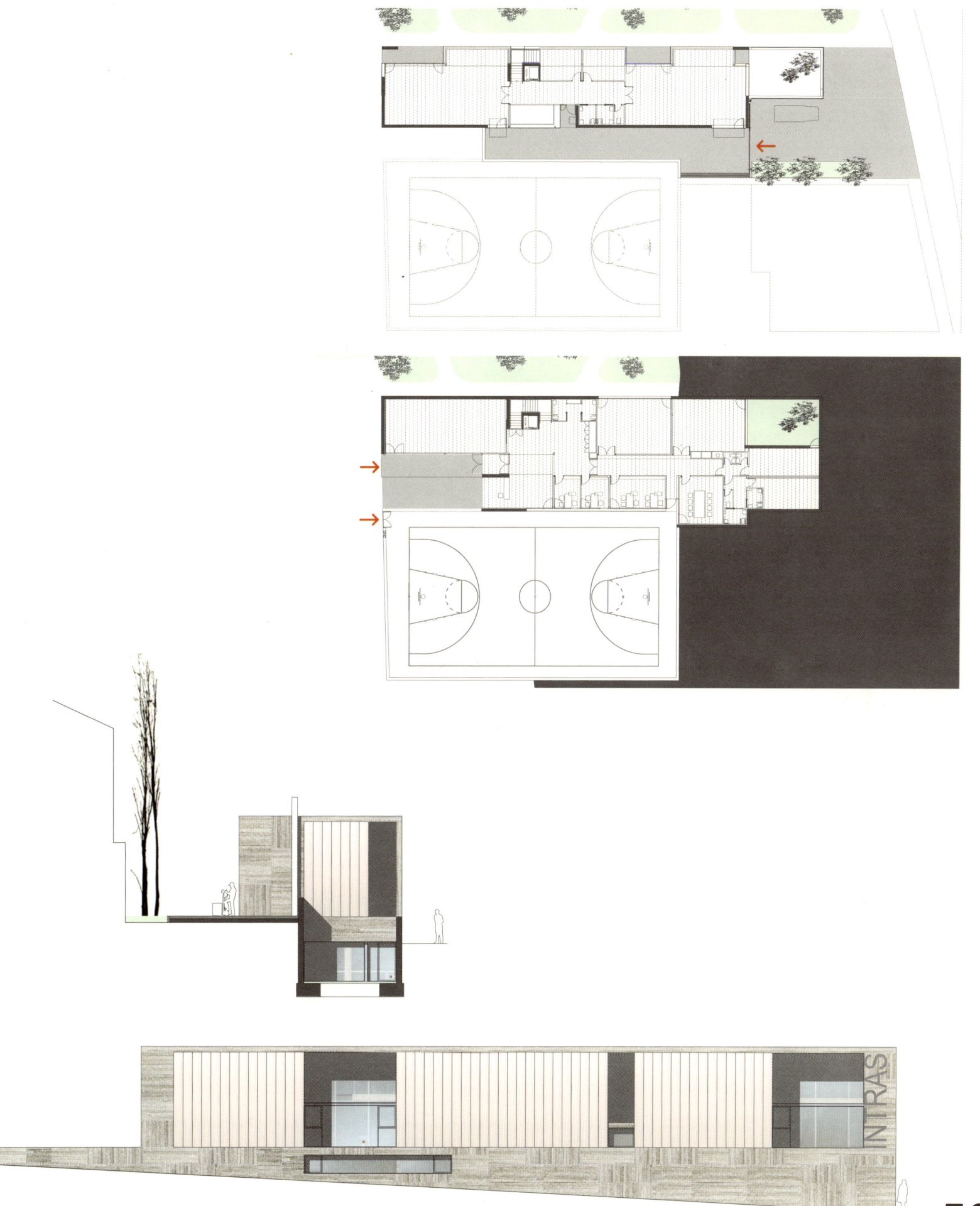

MOSQUITO COAST FACTORY

How can a cultural installation fit into an industrial site? Just dress it in a galvanized steel coat. Voilà!

Architects | Tolila+Gilliland Atelier d'Architecture
Project address | 5 rue de la Tamise ZAC Porte Estuaire, 44750 Campbon, France
Gross floor area | 515 m²
Main materials | galvanized steel, polycarbonate panels, polished concrete
Completion | 2012

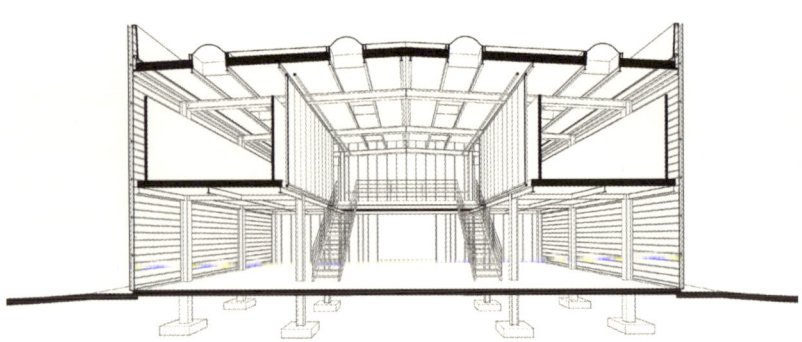

The question posed by the client was the possibility of a cultural island in an industrial site, the concrete fabrication of a utopic site for living, research and production. The cubic mass of galvanized steel echoes with the industrial façades of its environs; the monumental doors, only barely perceptible, sliding to disappear into the interior; the modularity of uses, the potential framework provided for the artist's future experimentations; the expression of the raw nature of materials; the great central nave and its lateral storage cells; the platform for exhibitions and the platform for living/sleeping; the affirmed symmetry, reinforced by two monumental stairs; the soft diffusion of light from the north façade in reference to artist's studios of the last century; the doors which open onto the landscape beyond; the simplicity of plan and the economy of means.

MOSQUITO
COAST
FACTORY

www.mosquitocoastfac

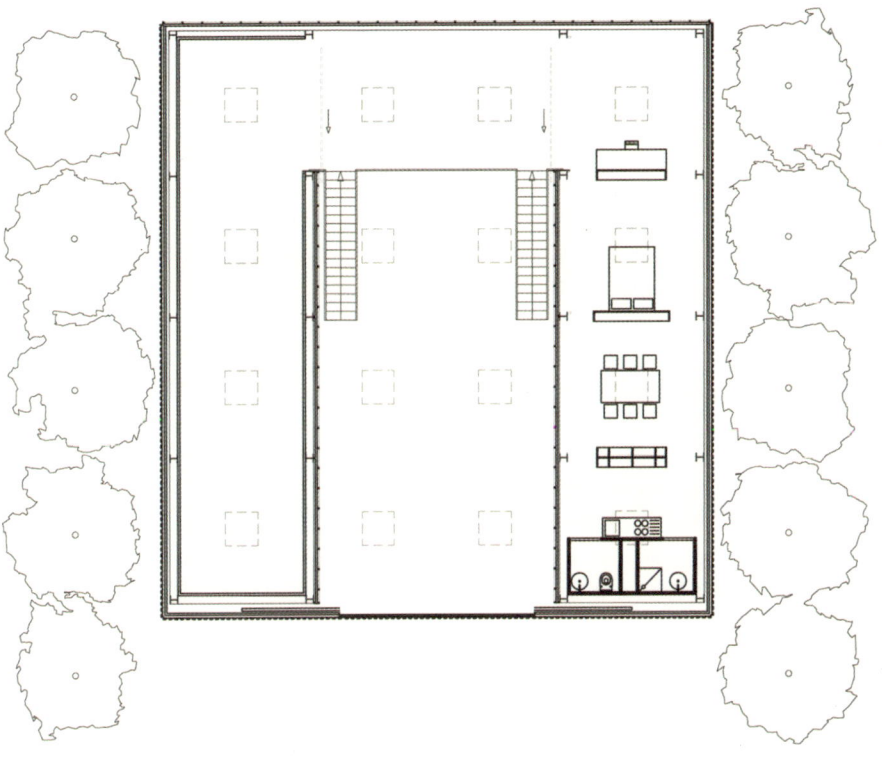

59

This project is located on Sopuchikoji, a small island at the top of Jeju Island. The client planned to construct condominiums and various auxiliary facilities on this site. Tadao Ando Architects were commissioned to design two of these facilities. The first was intended as a space where one can meditatively absorb the atmosphere of the island. Beyond the gate, water flows down over the stones, cleansing them. The Gate of Stone has a double-layer structure comprising a stone box and a concrete box. As visitors pass through the gate along the sloping path, they are distanced from every-day life and led into a deeply meditative space. The second part of the project is a restaurant sitting atop a cape. This building comprises a concrete volume divided into two parts, above which is a glass shaped box housing the observatory restaurant.

Gate of Stone

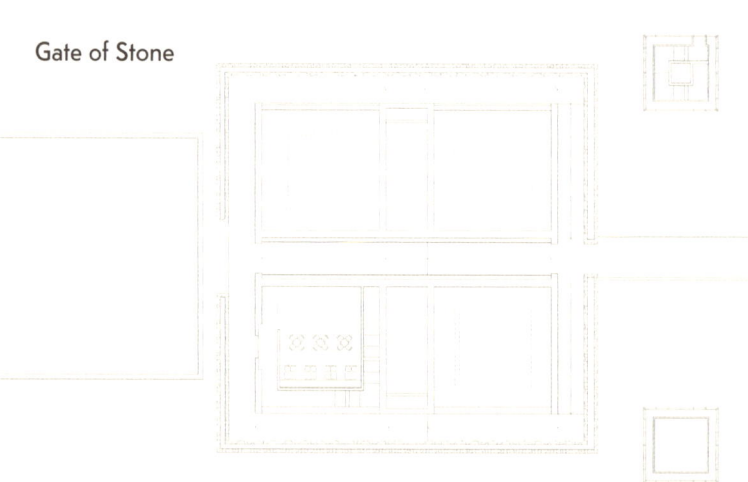

GATE OF STONE, GATE OF WIND

Air, water, earth: the natural elements come together to build a fortress behind the Gate of Stone; a meditative space on a South Korean island.

Architects | Tadao Ando Architect & Associates

Project address | Goseong-ri, Seongsan-eup, Seogwipo-si, Jeju-do, South Korea

Gross floor area | 1,302 m² (gate of stone), 2039 m² (gate of wind)

Main materials | stone, concrete

Completion | 2008

Gate of Wind

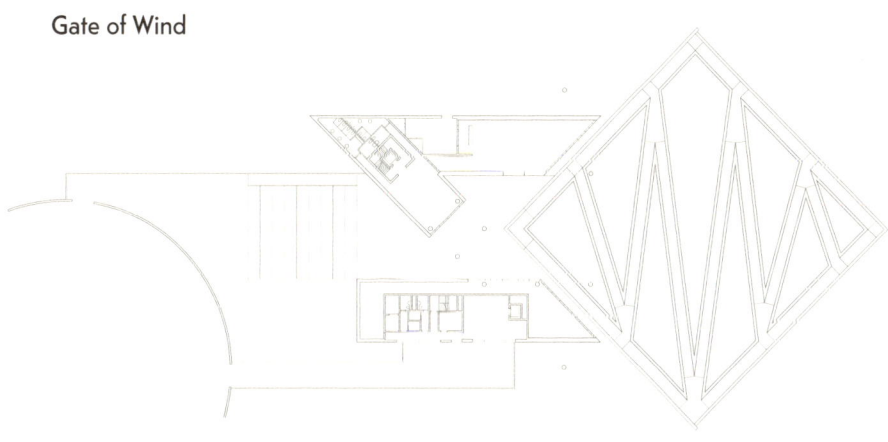

With panoramic views of the Pacific Ocean, Nobu's low horizontal profile hugs the bluff along famed Pacific Coast Highway in Malibu, CA. Architects and designers collaborated to create this noted sushi restaurant with a design blending Japanese notions of integration with the land and Californian openness. The palette of natural materials includes boardform concrete and bleached wood. Stone reflects light from clerestories and floor-to-ceiling window walls, further blurring boundaries between outside and inside. Wood-plank and decomposed-granite walkways wind through native plantings to shoji-screen inspired doors. Inside, dining nooks and continuous view corridors reinforce outdoor connection. Sheltered decks and interior fire features let diners enjoy beachfront views in elegance and comfort.

NOBU MALIBU

Mixing Japanese design with Californian nature –
the best of East and West form this elegant and
comfortable place.

Architects | Montalba Architects
Designers | Studio PCH
Project address | 22706 Pacific Coast Hwy, Malibu CA, USA
Gross floor area | 660 m²
Main materials | boardform concrete, bleached wood
Completion | 2012

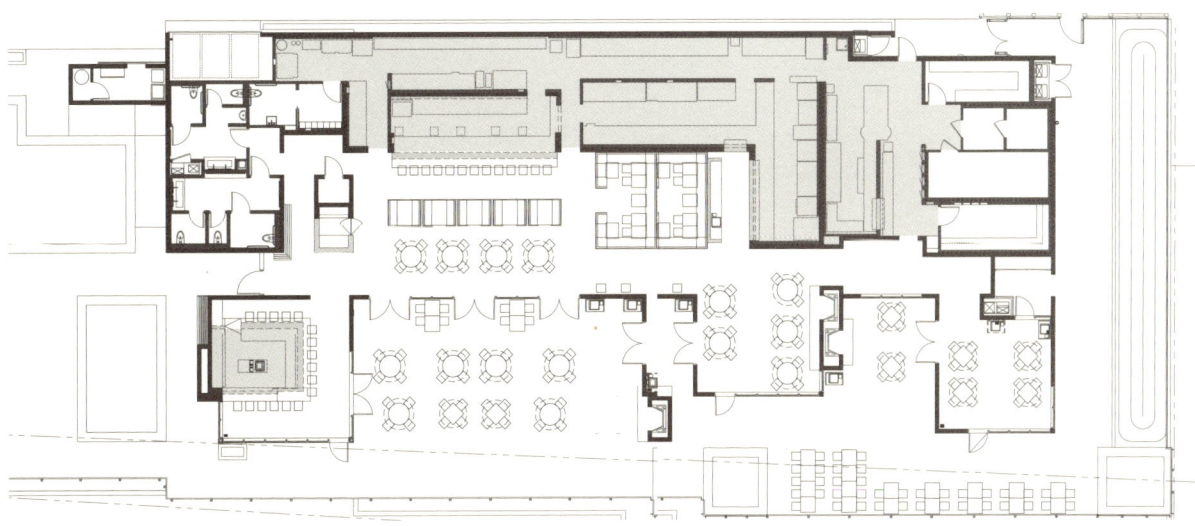

CHAPEL IN THE WOODS

Humble and sober; bricks and iron. Extreme architectural minimalism to achieve meditation.

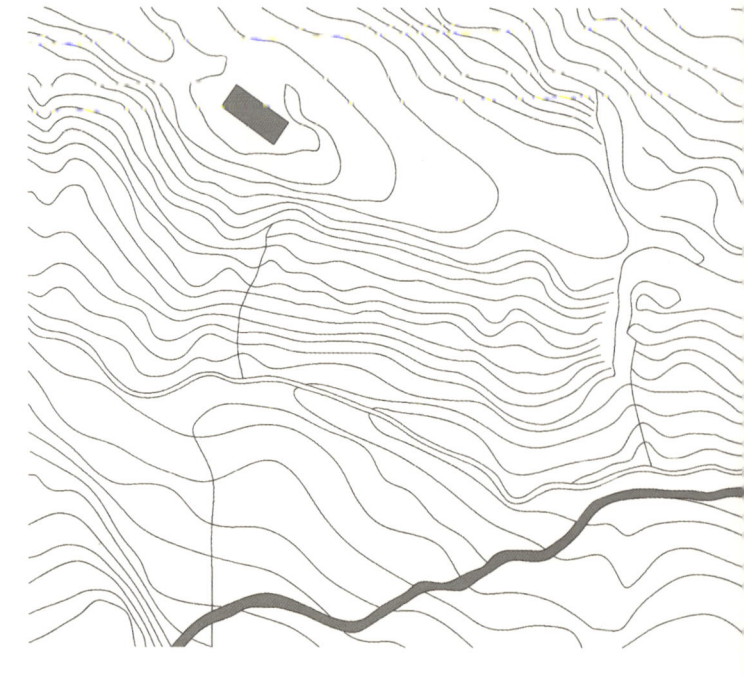

Architects | Paolo Zermani, Eugenio Tessoni
Project address | Varano dei Marchesi, Parma, Italy
Gross floor area | 200 m²
Main materials | iron, bricks
Completion | 2012

This intervention comprises a wall of just nine by six meters, which supports an iron cross of similar height, and a seat. The construction is composed of several elements that enhance the existing landscape morphology. Two symbolic elements, the wall and the cross, become a central feature. Each day, the morning sun illuminates the cross, gradually projecting the shadow onto the wall. The building is made of light pink bricks that are typical of this area, where clay kilns still exist today. The cross is made of rust-colored beams.

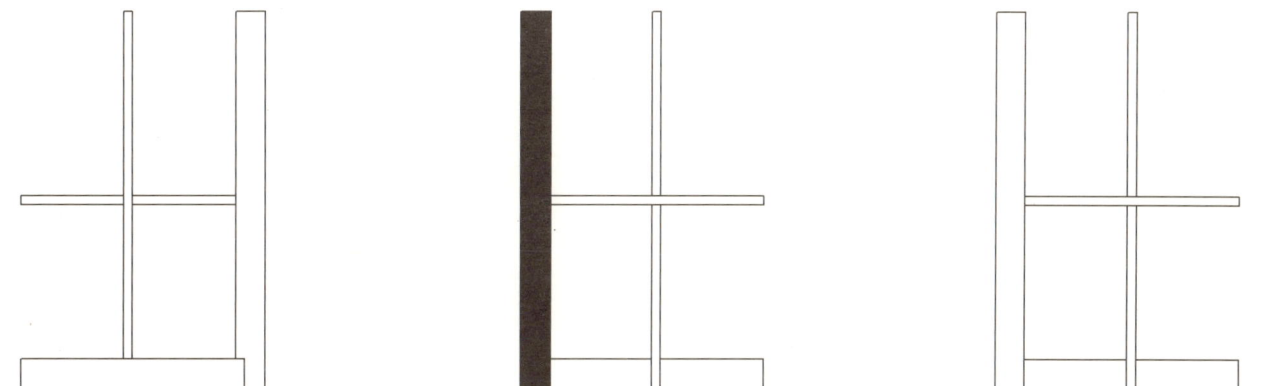

IMAGINATIVE

MINI

IMAGINATIVE

MINI

INNOVATIVE

INTR

IMPRESSIVE

INIMITABLE

IGUING

150-METER WEEKEND HOUSE

Thailand's next supermodel: a 150-meter long,
partially glazed body at the top of a hill; crowned
with a pool and a terrace on the roof.

Architects | Shinichi Ogawa & Associates
Project address | Thailand
Gross floor area | 1,592 m²
Main materials | concrete, wood
Completion | 2009

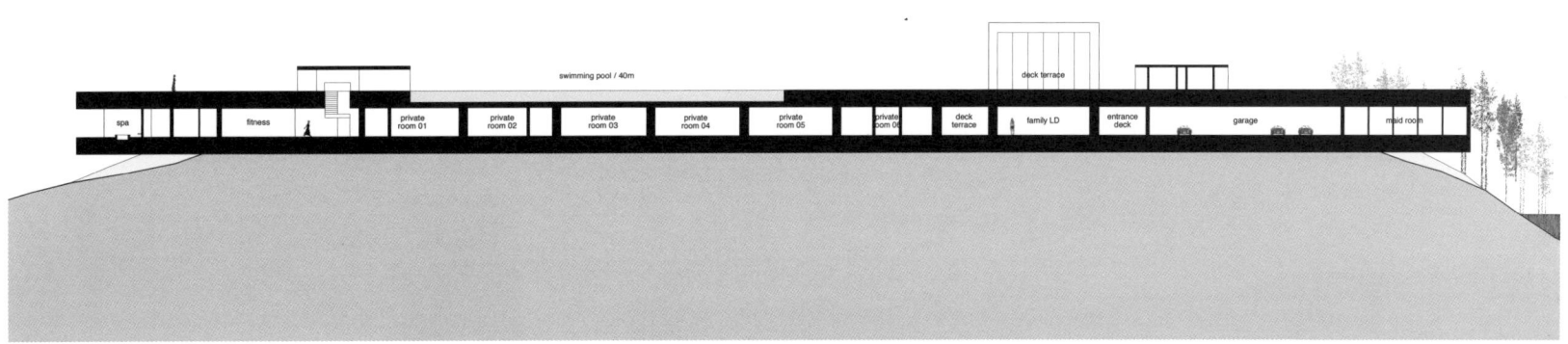

Overlooking the rich natural environment, this house tops a hill in a forest park in
Thailand. The main house is simply composed of a white cube and two horizontal
plates. All rooms are positioned linearly between the plates. A glazed room for
spa&fitness at the east end, six bedrooms with exclusive bathroom and living room,
a family living/dining room, and storage rooms at the west end. The length of the
house takes advantage of the beautiful landscape, gaining a panoramic view and
a dynamic terrace. At the same time, the design creates an airy comfortable living
environment. Above the private rooms, there is a roof top terrace covered with sand
and the swimming pool. The stairs from the hall below divides the large room into
southern living space and northern dining space.

Architects | Simon Freie Architekten
Project address | Stuhlsatzenhausweg, 66123 Saarbrücken, Germany
Gross floor area | 4,750 m²
Main materials | concrete, glass
Completion | 2009

This new building forms an integral part of the orthogonal architectural style of the campus. The height of the building matches that of the existing pharmacy faculty building to the west. The topography of the site varies in height, and this height differentiation has been solved by the addition of embankment walls. This solution allows natural ventilation and illumination of the rooms oriented towards the west. The entrance leads directly into the first, rather than the ground, floor. The foyer is located here and houses a central stairway and elevator. In the northern-most half of the building, two functional areas have been combined to form an open-plan laboratory, divided by moveable partitions. The division of the laboratory areas can be changed at a later date if desired, to suite various processes and working methods.

C2 3 PHARMACY RESEARCH BUILDING

What a harmonious and luminous building! No waste of space or time – the perfect place for research.

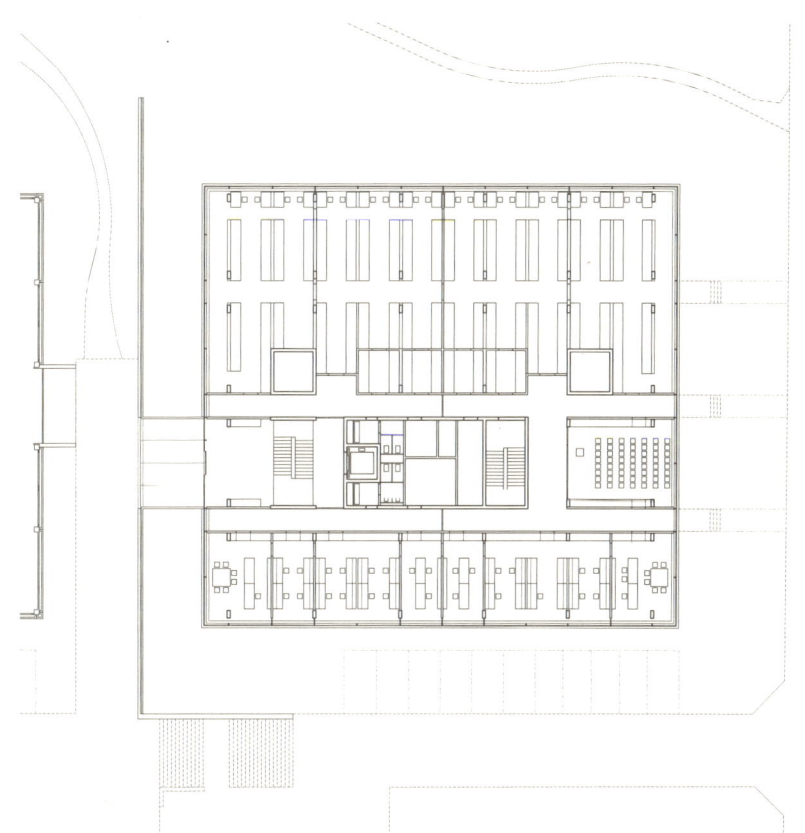

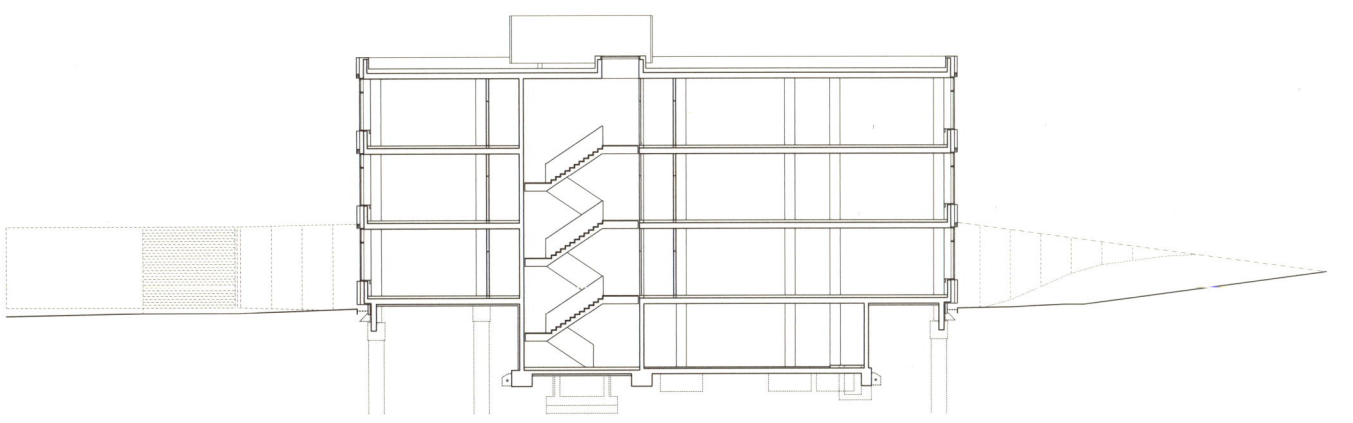

The romantic image of ruins, so often rejected for being nostalgic and anachronistic, is nonetheless able to convey not only the evocative power of buildings from the past but also the destructive strength of time and nature. This project unveils the floor plan of an underground museum, which articulates its halls around a sequence of solid and void spaces, covered areas and courtyards that guide visitors along their route. The main lobby leads to a large courtyard with a square floor plan, around which the main public spaces are organized. A deep, elongated courtyard articulates the private-use areas: administration, conservation workshops, and research zones. A final courtyard is the expansion of the museum exhibition areas toward the exterior. The conception of the project allows for further expansion, making it possible to add pavilions if needed. The new museum establishes almost imperceptibly a permanent dialogue with the architecture and the landscape of the old Arab medina.

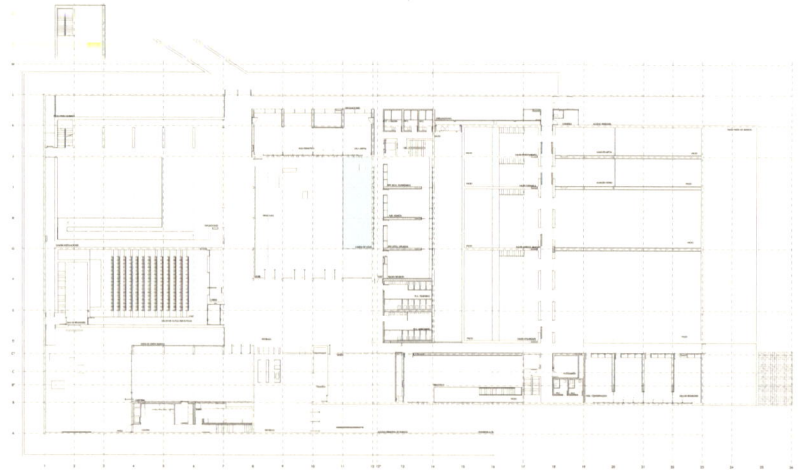

MADINAT AL ZAHRA MUSEUM

What is hidden behind these thick concrete walls?
Enter and experience the history of the ancient
caliphate city Madinat al-Zahra.

Architects | Nieto Sobejano Arquitectos
Project address | Carretera Palma del Río, 14071 Córdoba, Spain
Gross floor area | 9,125 m²
Main materials | concrete, corten steel
Completion | 2009

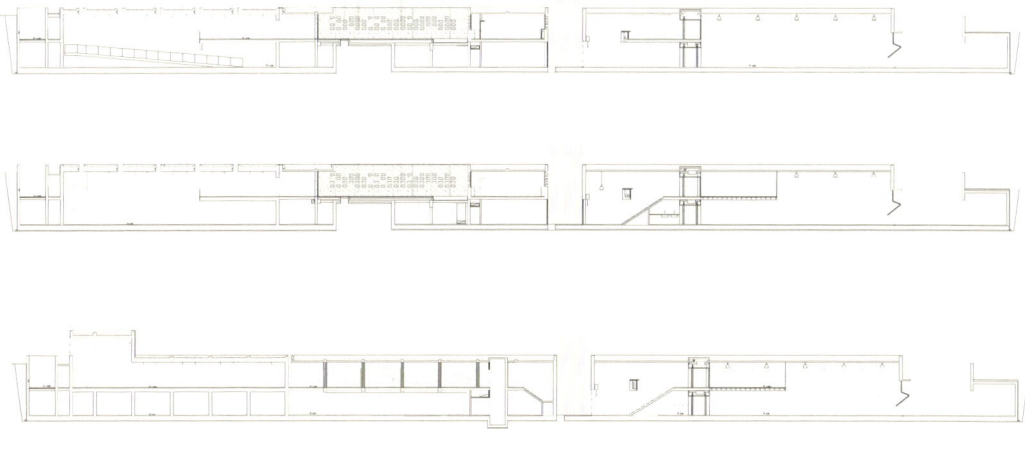

The design of this house develops from the client's concerns about limiting excessive heat from sunlight at the front of the house, which faces west, and about how to optimize the flow of air through the house. A wide staircase has been built at the center of the house, thus allowing a gently breeze to flow down through the entire house. An inbuilt table is positioned at the top of the staircase, providing a cool, bright and airy space for the inhabitants to sit. The rooms on the second floor are arranged around the staircase. The architects restricted the size of the front windows in order to provide some respite from the sun, opening these windows allows sunlight to reflect off the lower portion of the staircase, providing illumination from the bottom up.

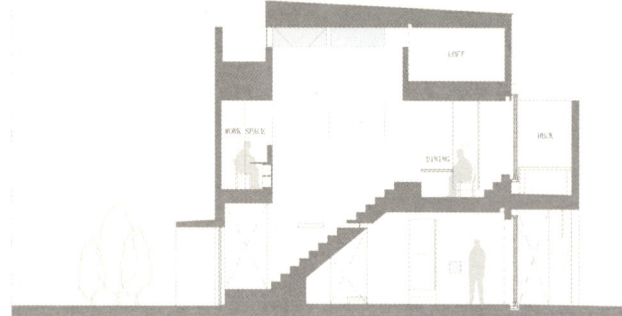

HOUSE IN HAKUSAN

Step by step on the way to home sweet home...

Architects | Fujiwara-Muro architects
Project address | Hakusan-shi, Ishikawa, Japan
Gross floor area | 95 m²
Main materials | wood, concrete
Completion | 2011

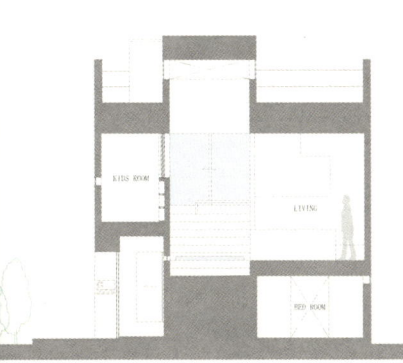

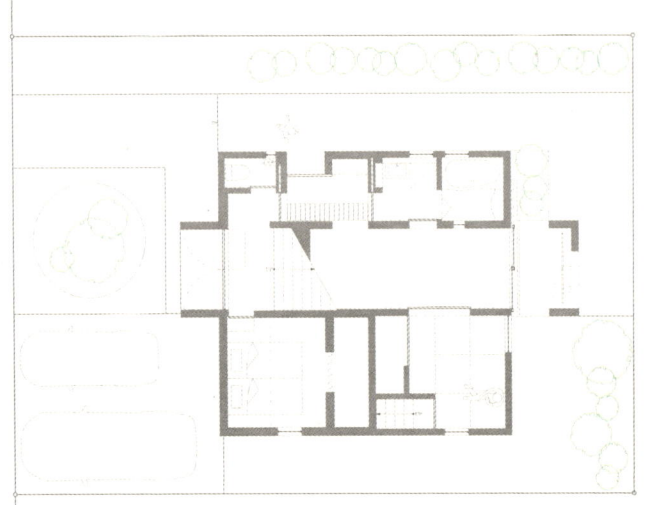

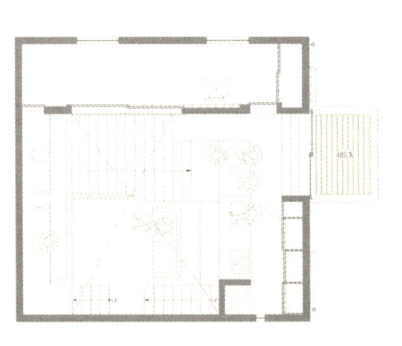

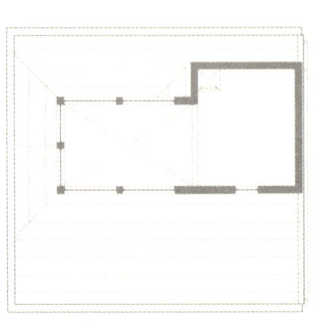

This house is located near the northern coast of Zealand, Denmark. The plot is the result of the partitioning of a larger plot belonging to an old, thatched house. The two buildings at each end of the site, are inhabited by two generations and the layout of the site plan was careful to provide both with separate and shared spaces. The main architectural focus concentrated on adding space and light to the relatively small area. The plan separates the bedrooms from the living space and introduces an open hallway. In working with the section, the ceiling height was minimized to give contrast to the "sky-boxes" that add space and air.

SKYBOX HOUSE

A liaison of open and closed, light and dark. 75 square meters of finest Danish architecture expertise.

Architects | Primus architects/David Bülow-Jacobsen and Per Appel
Project address | Kodriverengen 4A, 3390 Nødebohuse, Denmark
Gross floor area | 75 m²
Main materials | wood
Completion | 2009

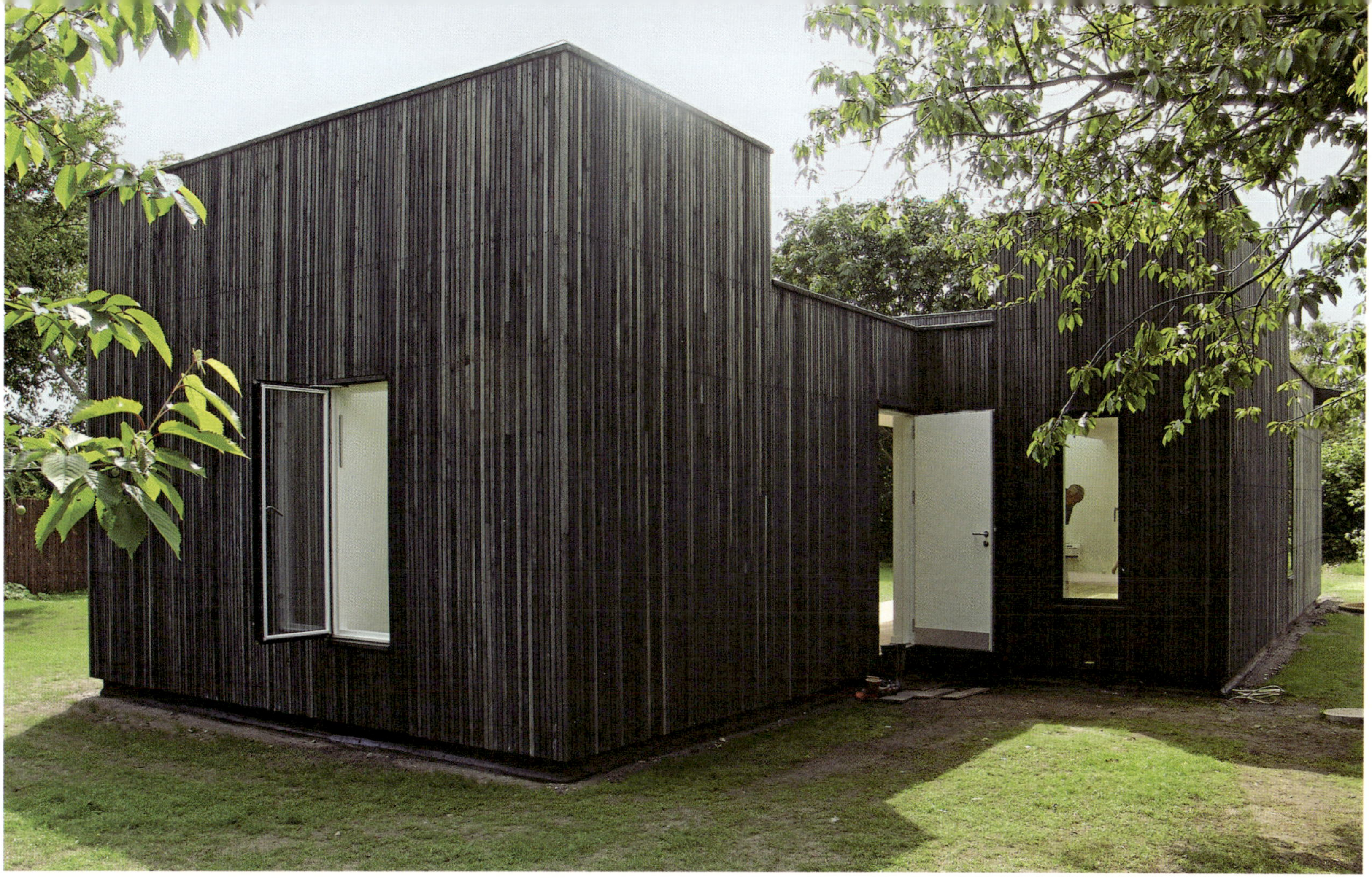

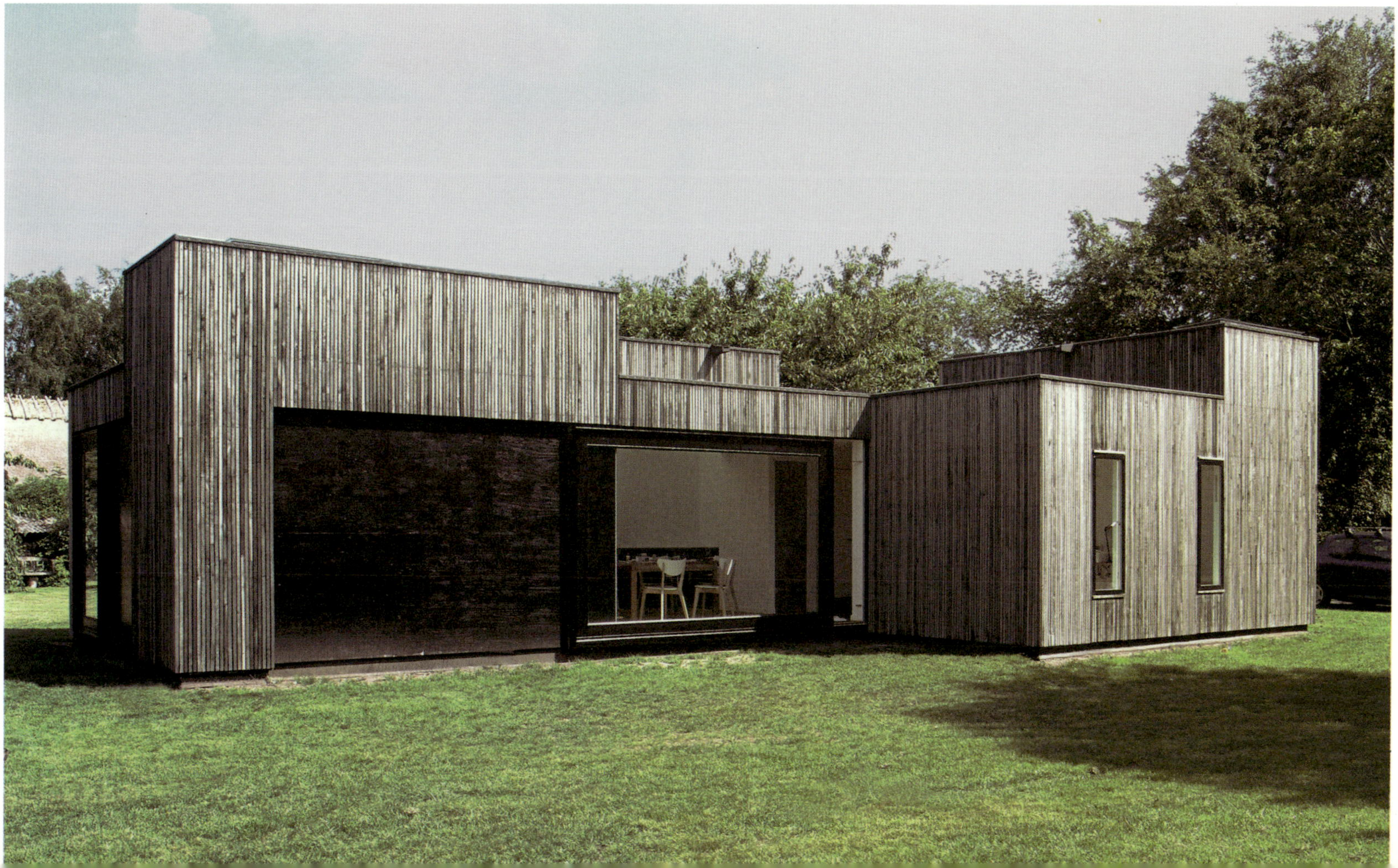

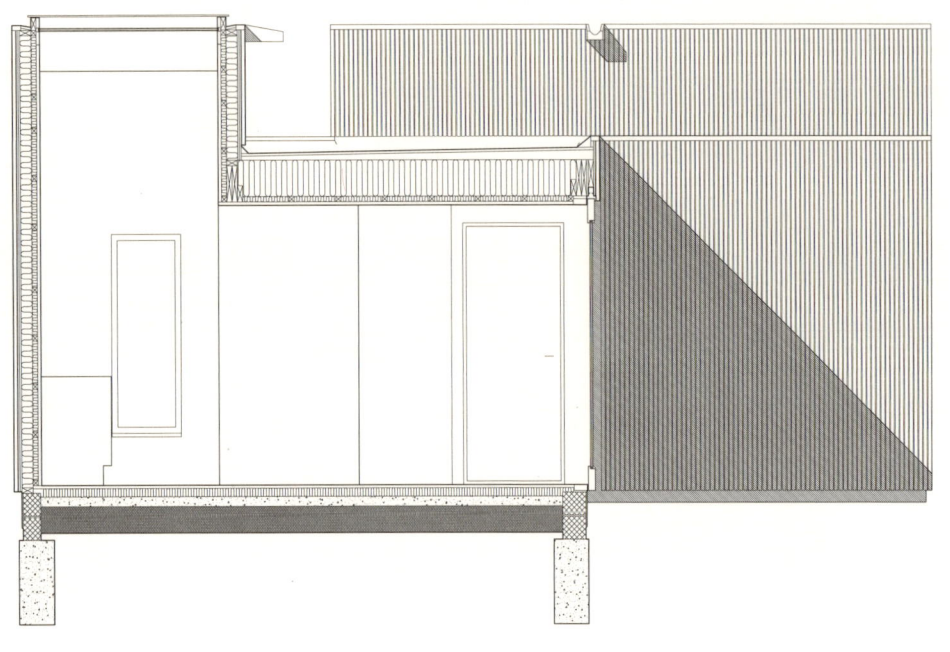

HOUSE ON THE CORNER

The challenge: to build a 72-square-meter house on an unusually small and irregular street corner. The solution: connect and stack all areas.

Architects | Keizo Matsuda Architect with Masatoshi Fujimoto
Lighting designer | Junko Kusano
Project address | Osaka 562–0031, Japan
Gross floor area | 76 m²
Main materials | concrete, wood
Completion | 2012

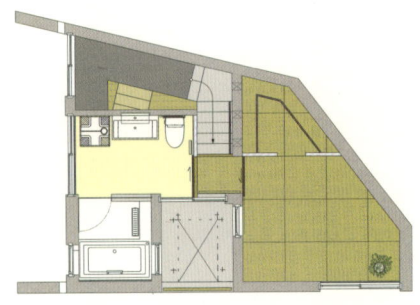

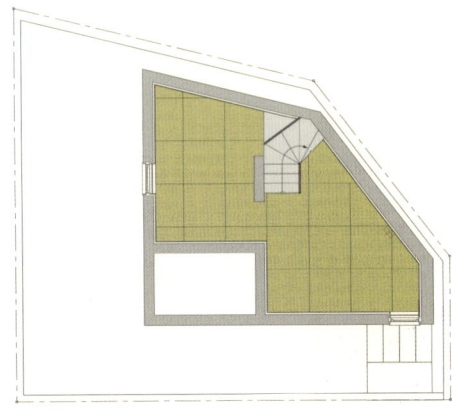

This house is located in a new residential neighborhood in the northern suburb of Osaka, Japan. The site presented the architect with a challenge, as it was considered to be unusable, as it is unusually small and irregular in shape. Because of local regulations, the total floor area of the house is limited to 76 square meters, which is extremely small even for Japanese living standards. In order to maximize the spatial experience, the kitchen, dining and living areas are all efficiently connected, with the sense of division achieved by staggered floors. The client expressed a wish that the house be very private. The architect's response was to express the street sides as a protected shell and without any openings, thus giving the house a sculptural appearance. In contrast, the house is very transparent on the other sides to allow natural light to flow inside.

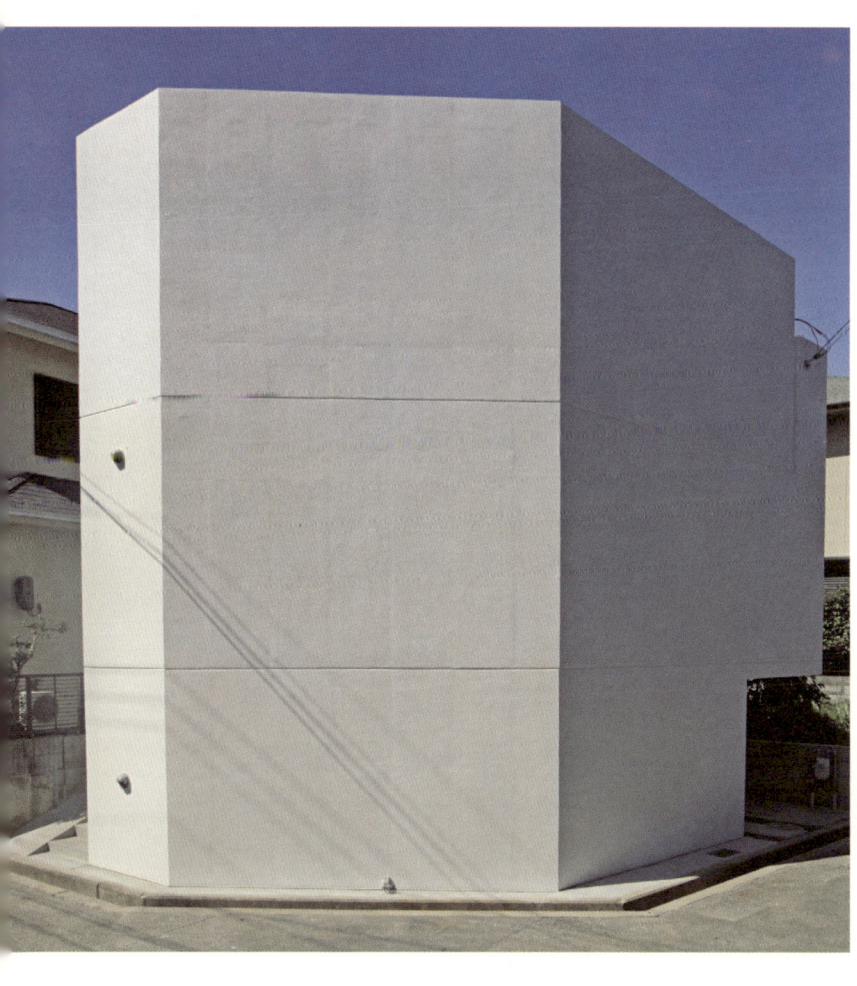

103

BEAUTY SALON

Welcome and feel at home! The house-shaped entrance to this beauty salon is an invitation to wellbeing and coziness.

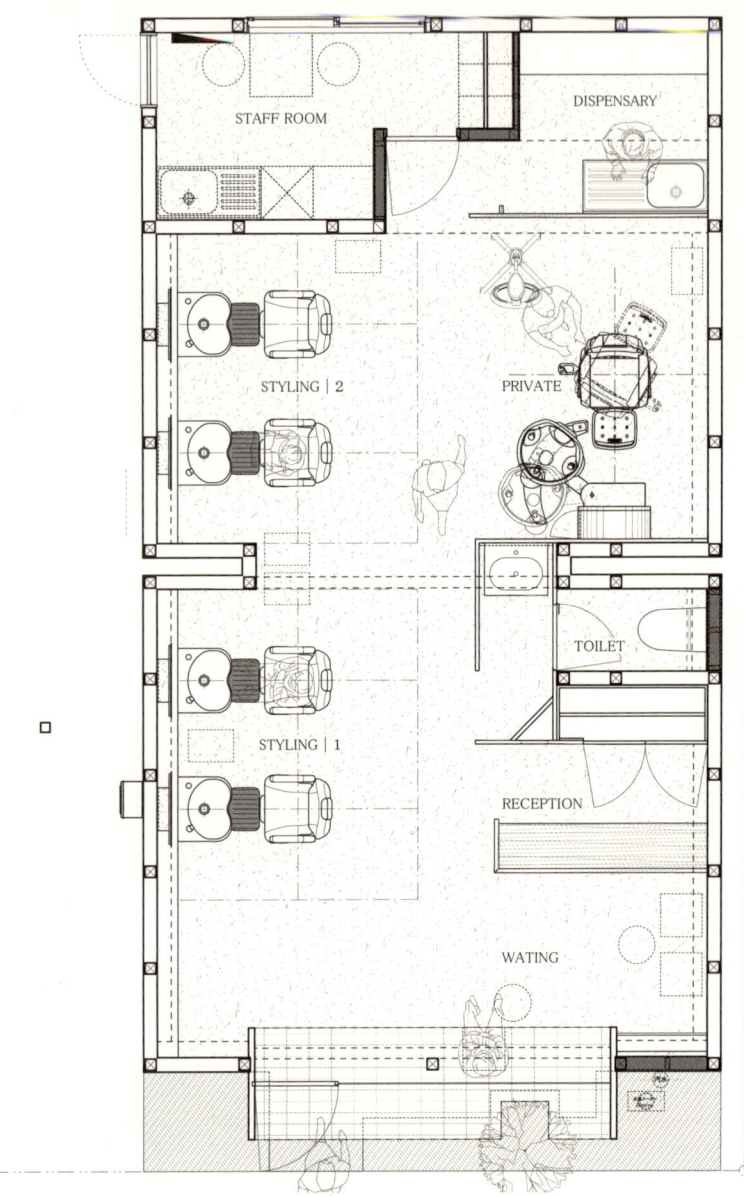

STAFF ROOM

DISPENSARY

STYLING | 2

PRIVATE

STYLING | 1

TOILET

RECEPTION

WATING

Architects | Tsubasa Iwahashi | Architects
Project address | 1-1-3 mokuzaicho-higashi, sakai-ku, sakai, Osaka 590-094, Japan
Gross floor area | 55 m²
Main materials | plaster, wood
Completion | 2013

This elegant beauty salon uses a simple and classic design to attract customers, rather than using of a typical and brightly lit storefront. The design blends with the surroundings, sharing a dialogue with nearby buildings. The entrance is shaped like the outline of a house, and is intended as a welcoming gesture, inviting customers to come in and to feel at home. The interior is characterized by a linear and clear design, the edges and lines of which are emphasized by white light, opening the interior out and making it visible from the outside.

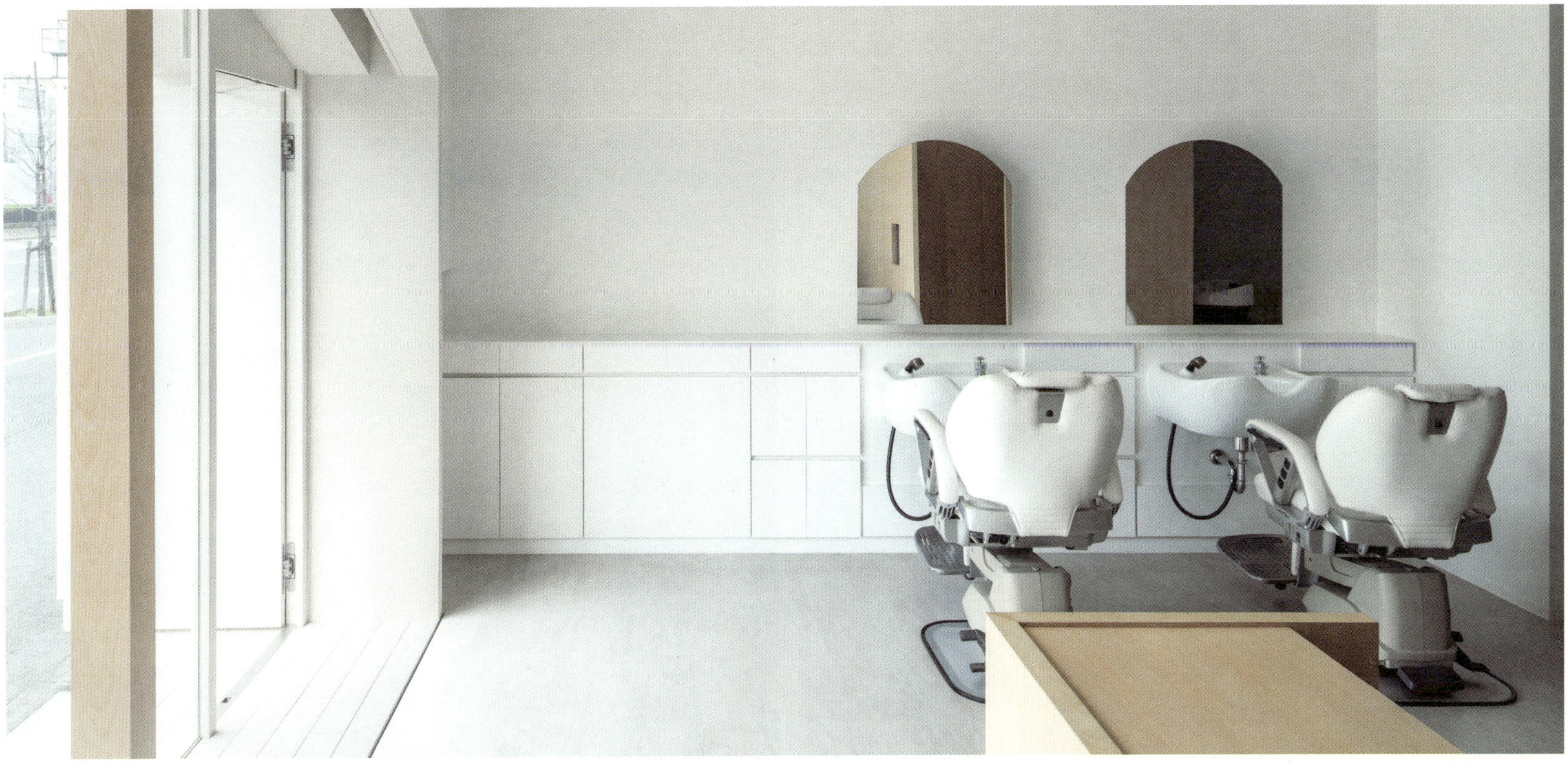

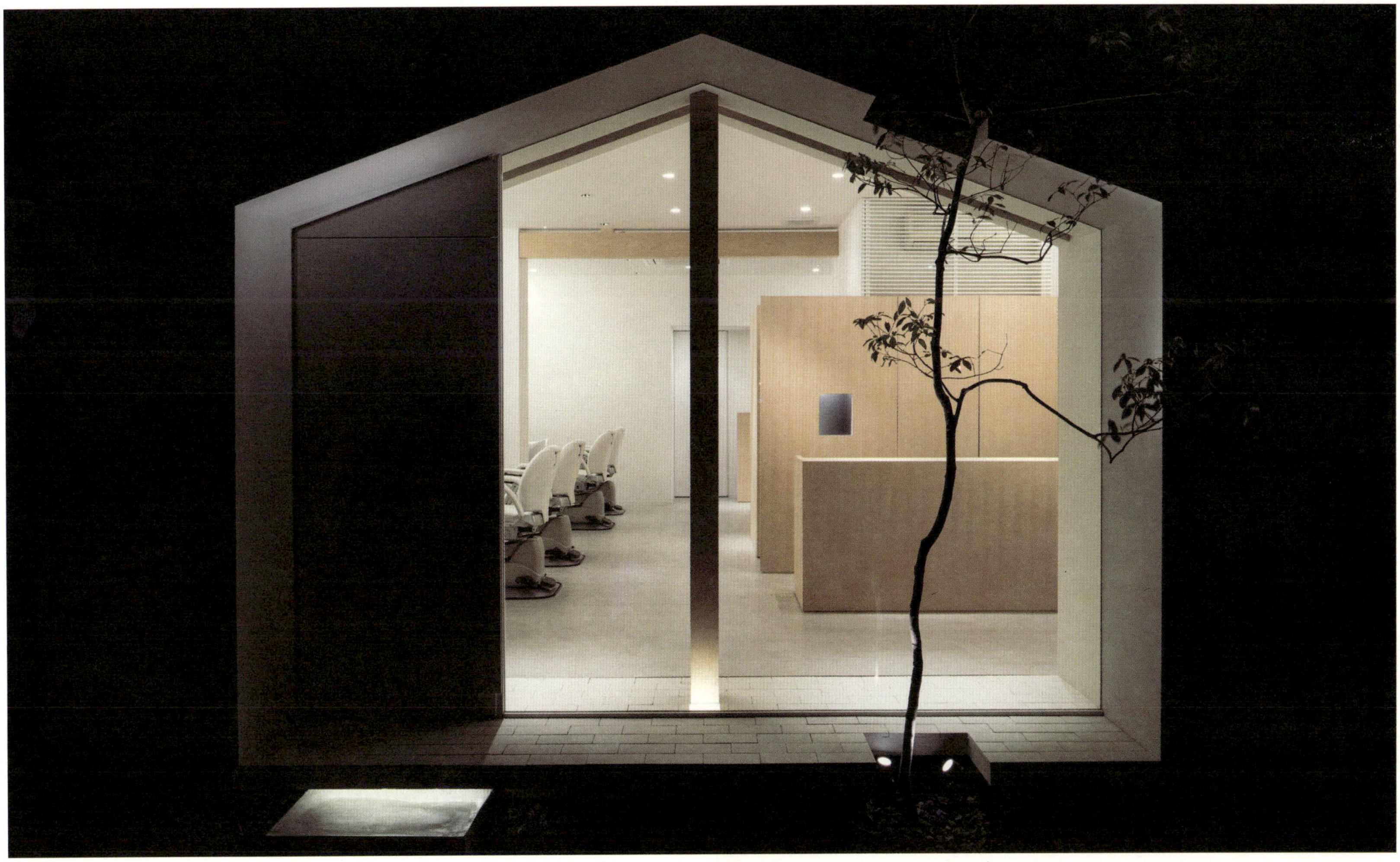

MINIMALIST HOUSE

Extreme simplicity creates extreme intimacy:
The house as a bulwark between private and
public spheres.

Architects | Shinichi Ogawa & Associates
Project address | Itoman, Okinawa, Japan
Gross floor area | 102 m²
Main materials | concrete, limestone
Completion | 2009

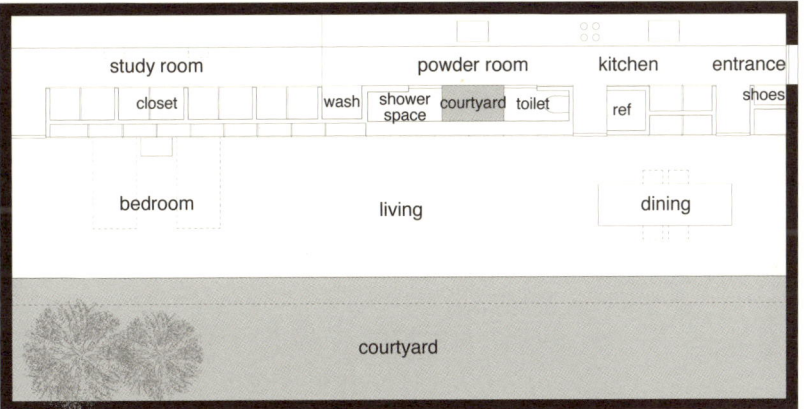

study room · closet · powder room · kitchen · entrance · wash · shower space · courtyard · toilet · ref · shoes · bedroom · living · dining · courtyard

This building is a courtyard house for a couple in Itoman-shi, Okinawa, Japan. The house is built on a three-grid design and comprises four vertical plates, which form the exterior walls, and one horizontal plate as a roof slab. A functional layout has been created by inserting a void of three by 18 meters, which forms the courtyard for the house. The division of the house into two areas characterizes the space composition. The first area comprises the living room, dining room, and bedroom, while the second is composed of the kitchen, powder room, and study room. The internal space has eaves that control the amount of direct sunlight entering the house. The functional counter unit incorporated into the kitchen, powder room, and study is made of DuPont Corian.

109

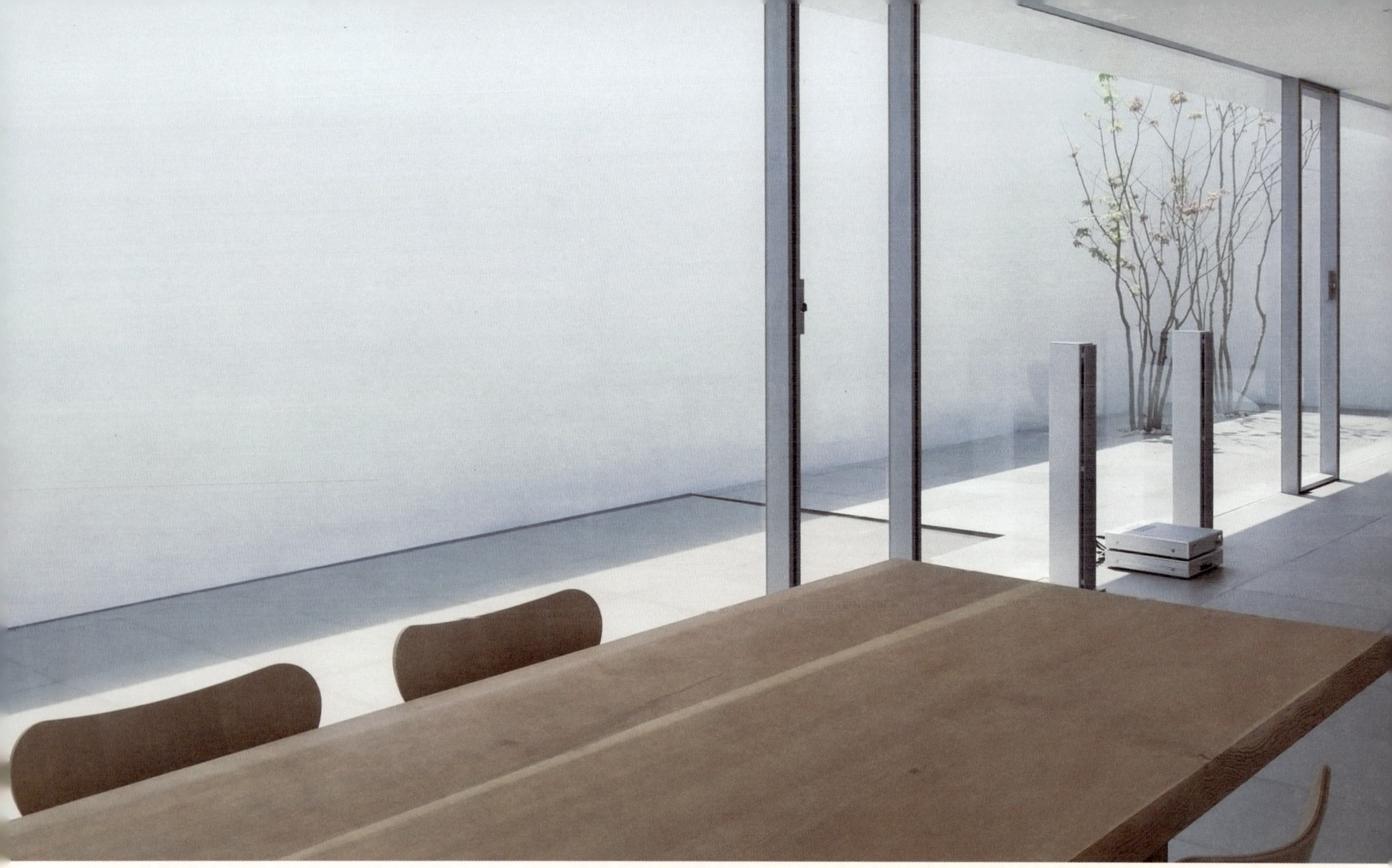

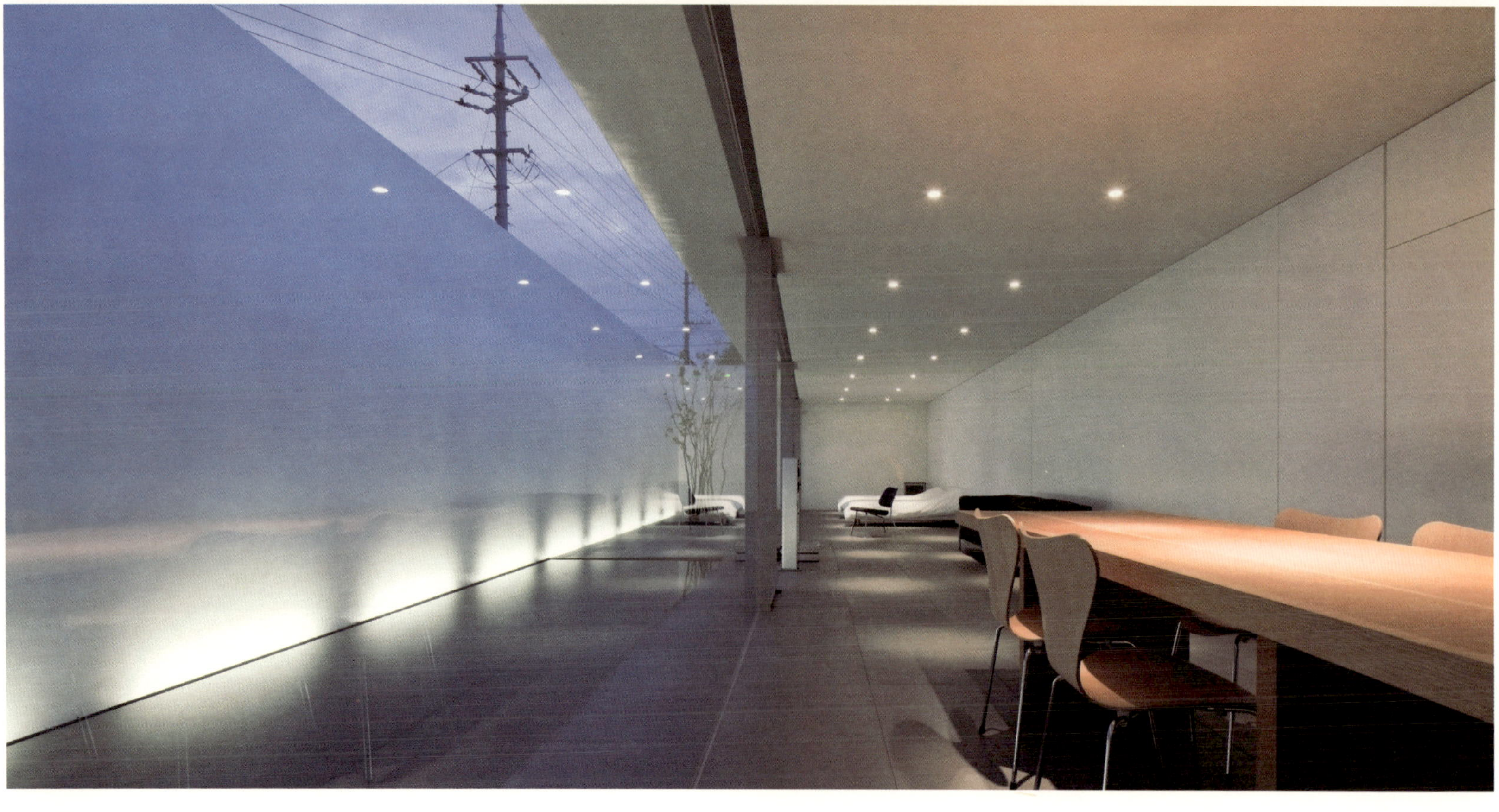

Architects | AZL Architects
Project address | XiXi Wetland, Hangzhou, Zhejiang Province, China
Gross floor area | 4,000 m²
Main materials | concrete
Completion | 2011

Located near the wetlands west of central Hangzhou, the Xixi Artists' Club is laid out like a village with five units. Each cluster relies on three Y-shaped volumes in two sizes, capped with six- and three-square-meter frameless windows, creating panoramas of the surrounding landscape. Twisting fiberglass installations work with the cubic structure to redefine internal spaces and join walls, floors, and ceilings together. The larger six-meter-tall structure is concrete, while the smaller sections sport translucent white PVC panels to diffuse direct sunlight. The confrontation between the oblique with the linear, the translucent panels with the concrete, and the external shape with the interior installations create a heightened sense of space.

XIXI ARTISTS' CLUB HOUSE

Bright white lanterns on the horizon of the wild Hangzhou wetlands. Contemporary design meets perfect working conditions in this artists' village.

112

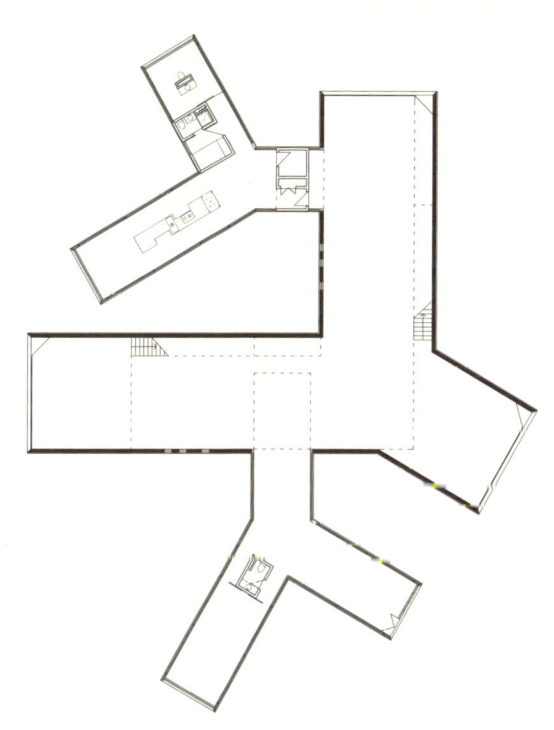

This project is located in downtown Miyazaki, Japan. The road in front of the project location is very busy and noisy, and there are tall residential buildings to the south. Whilst considering all these factors, the architect came up with the idea of wrapping the new building in a white envelope, thus separating it from the crowded location, while allowing sunlight to flow into the courtyard, making the interior much lighter and brighter. The house makes a calm and quiet impression, defying the busy surrounding and presenting quiet face to passersby.

Architects | Michiya Tsukano/Tsukano Architect Office
Project address | Miyazaki, Japan
Gross floor area | 108 m²
Main materials | concrete
Completion | 2012

HOUSE-T

A sudden need for calm and privacy in big city life?
Live like a turtle and take refuge under the white
protective shell.

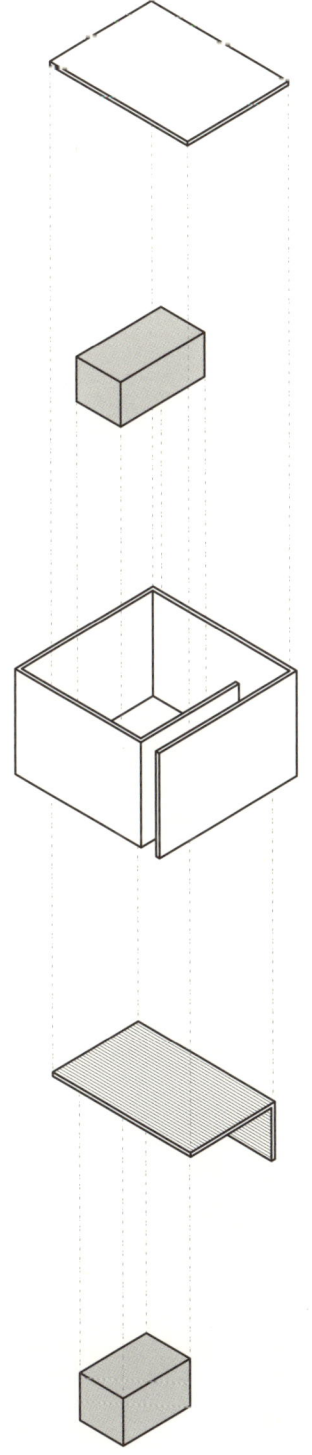

dining
court
kitchen
study

living
bedroom
bathroom

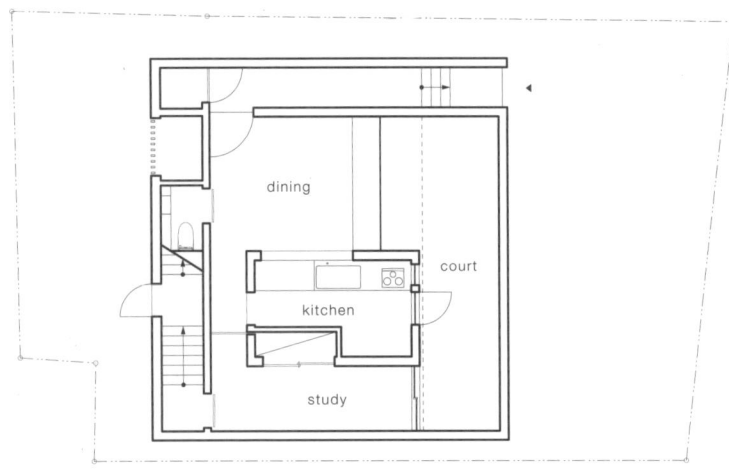

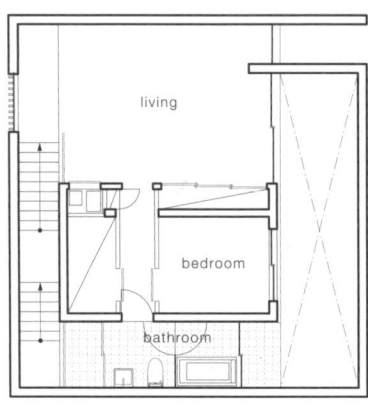

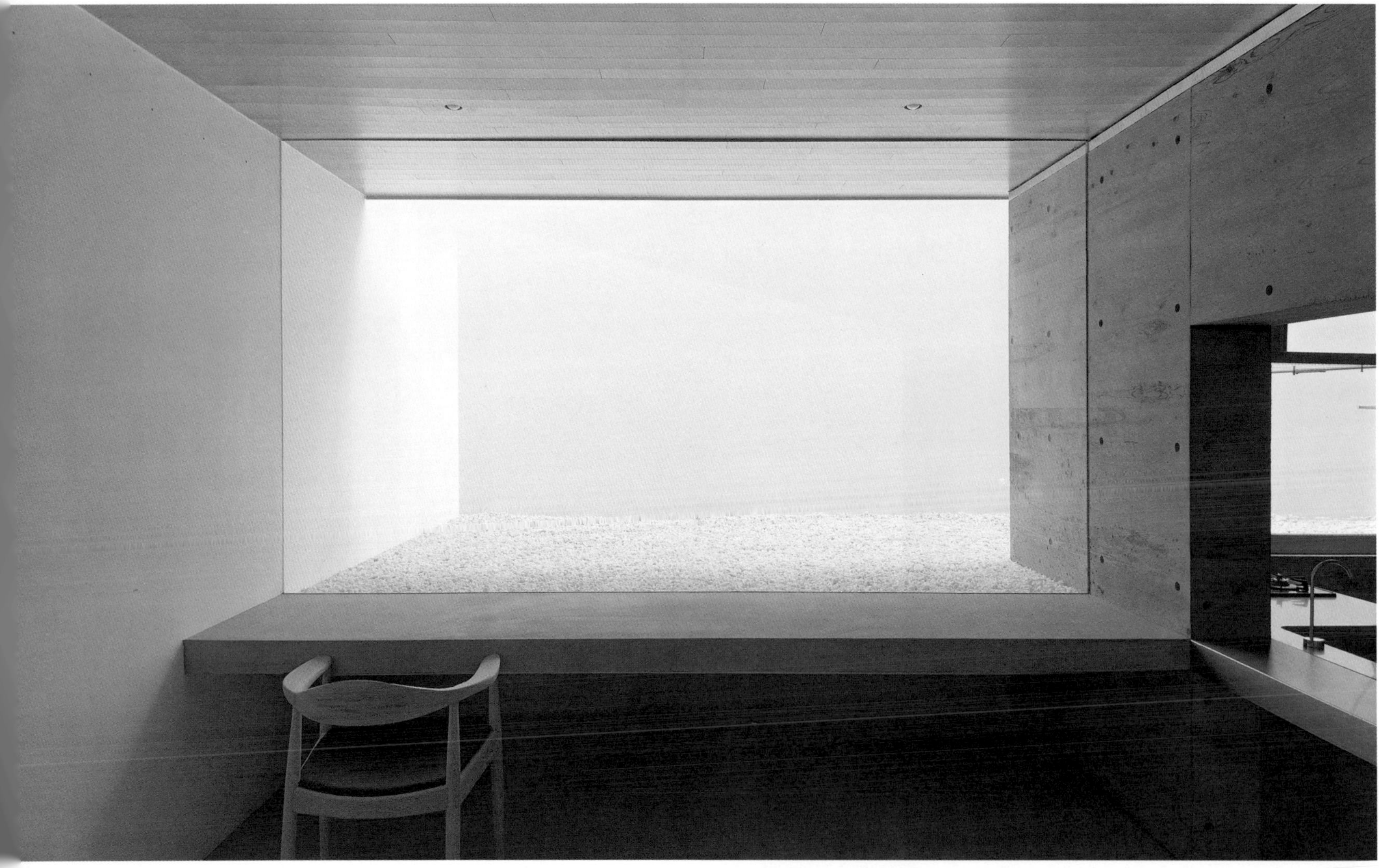

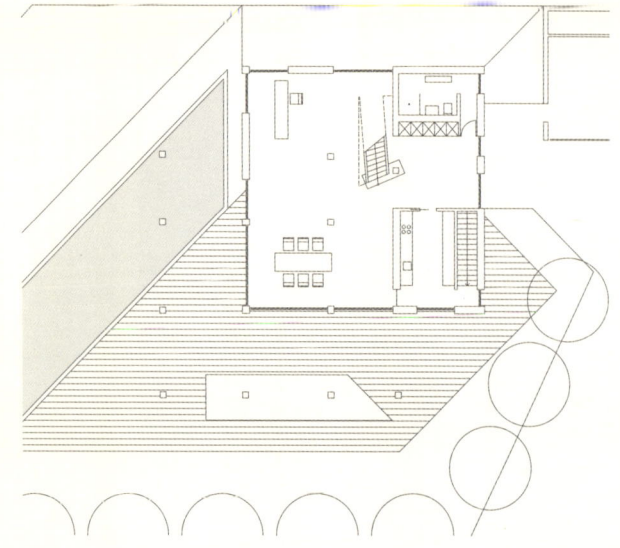

Nothing in the design of this cubic building distracts from fundamental actions like sleeping, reading, eating, writing, talking to friends, thinking and being. Everything is clear, transparent, precise, and unadulterated. Silence is used as a contrast to consumer society and the stimulus satiation of the modern world. Minimalism is expressed by a minimum of components used throughout the design. Empty space, pure white Thassos marble, white pine, clear glass, white linen and white-painted plaster characterize the entire design. The exact details are so reduced that they are barely noticeable as individual features, but are rather perceived as a whole.

HOUSE G

It is all about light and harmony... Take a break
from everyday life and relax.

Architects | Brandl Architekten
Project address | Regensburg, Germany
Gross floor area | 280 m²
Main materials | white pine
Completion | 2011

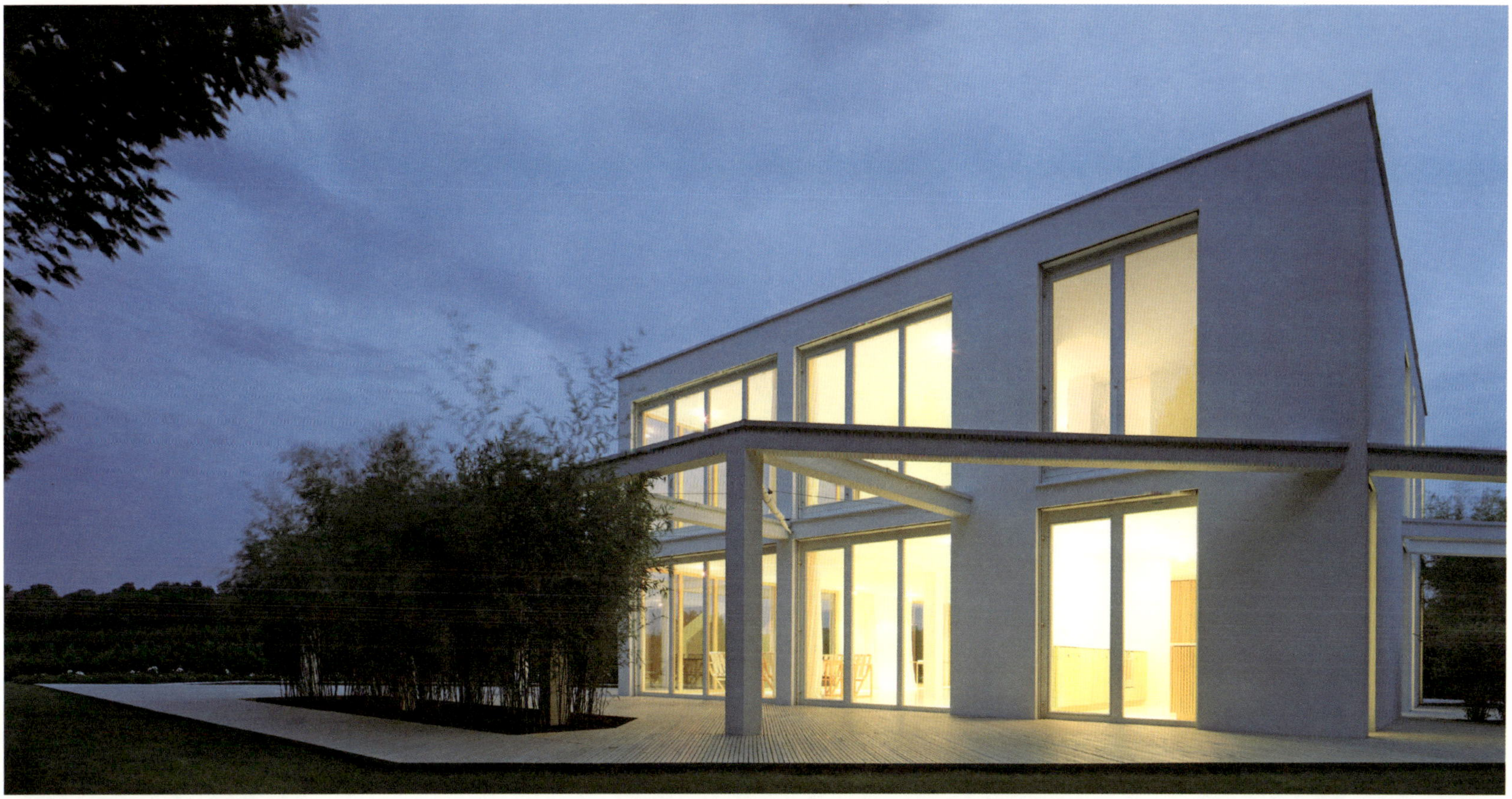

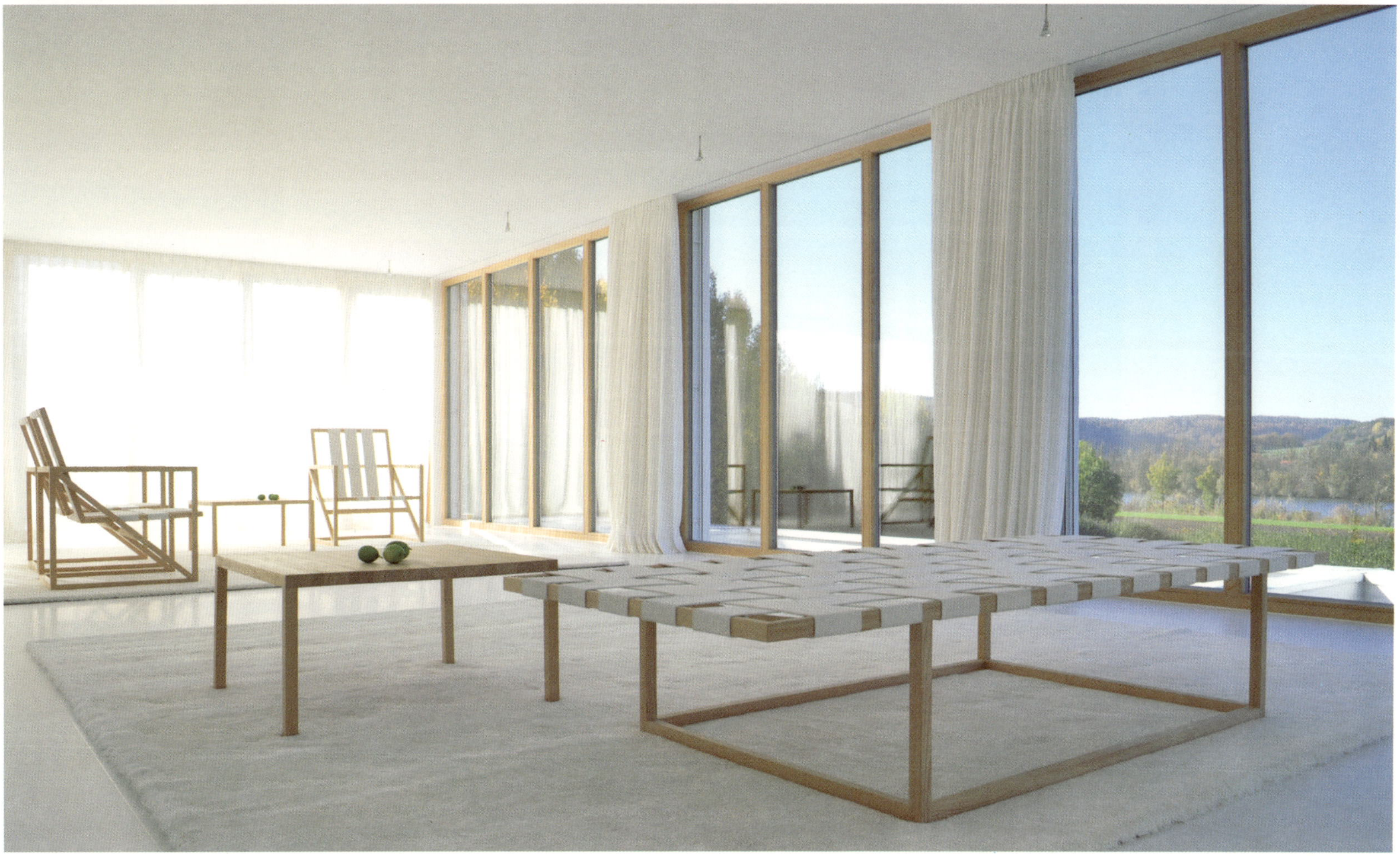

HOUSE K

House K turns the senses inside out! Nature fits into architecture and forms a harmonious landscape of interior-exterior spaces.

Architects | Titus Bernhard Architekten
Project address | confidential
Gross floor area | 375 m²
Main materials | concrete
Completion | 2012

This family home broaches the issue of the transition between interior and exterior and the targeted positioning of openings to emphasize the beautiful views and to fade out the neighboring properties. The complex cubature of the house with its skylights and atriums, as well as a large terrace with pool, allow for a smooth transition from the house to the garden. The spatial arrangement is characterized by the contrast between light and dark, architecture and nature. The forms and styles of the classical Modern style are used throughout. The interconnectedness of the architecture and landscape give the house its autonomy. Materials are limited to fine-grain white marble plaster, warm light sandstone, and glass.

125

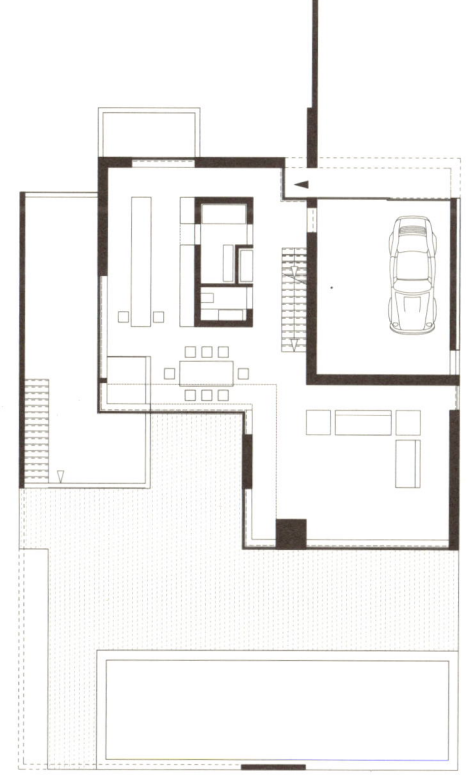

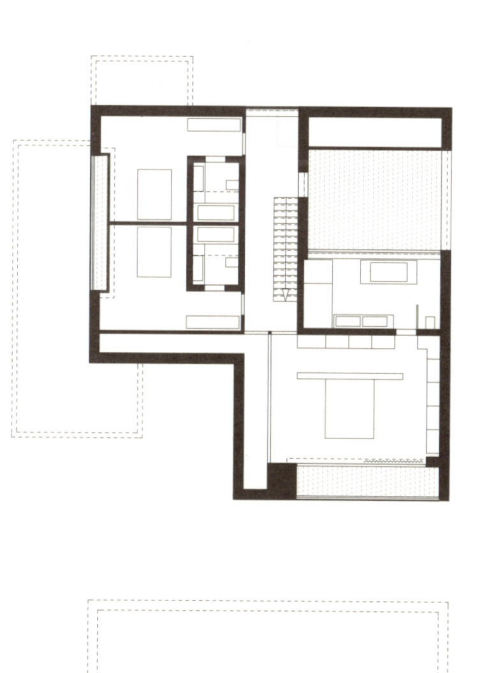

NUDE

NEAT

MINI

NONCO

NOTICEABLE

NFORMIST

NOBLE

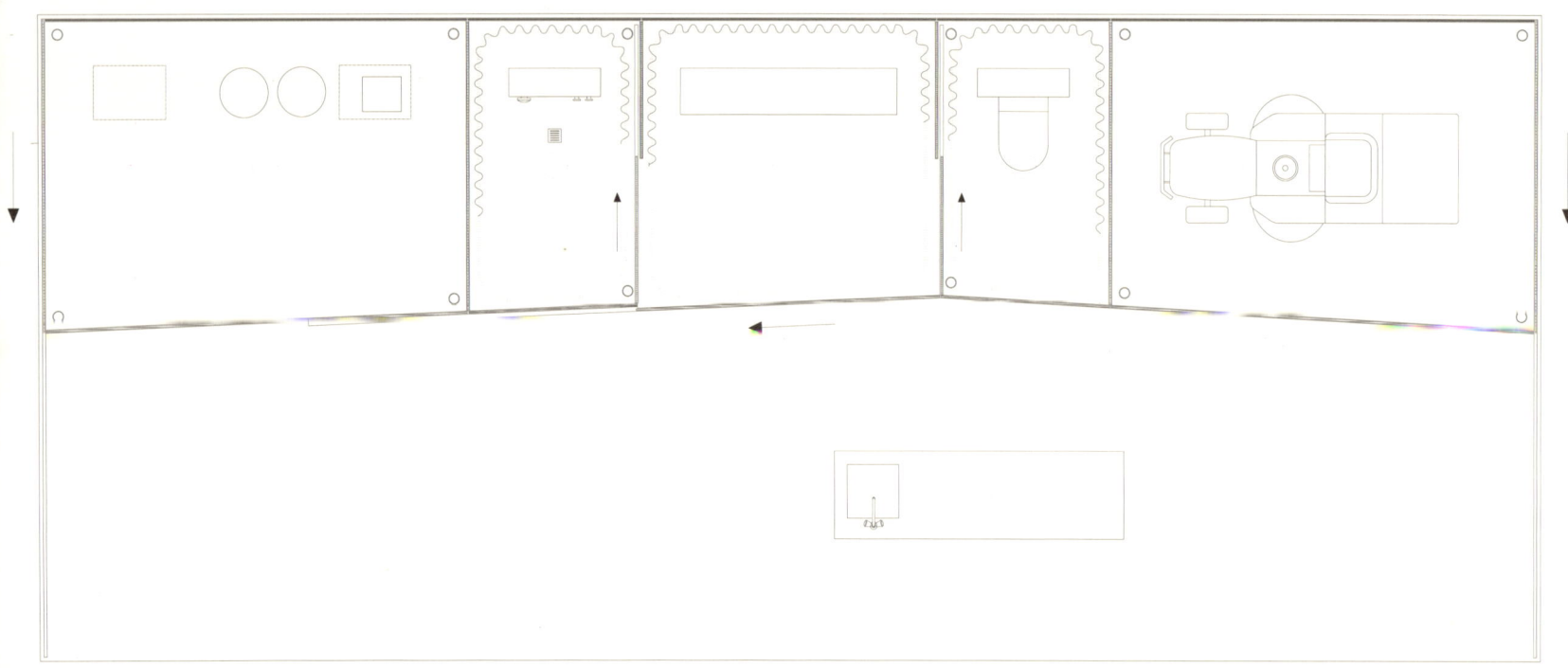

POOL HOUSE

A pool house does not only have to be functional,
it can also be elegant.

Architects | Baumhauer
Project address | Munich, Germany
Gross floor area | 25 m²
Main materials | glass
Completion | 2010

This pavilion combines space for the lawnmower, pool equipment, storage space, shower, WC, changing facilities and a bar. The pavilion can be opened out by means of three large sliding doors. The equipment is stored behind the glass façade, the lines and edges of which dissolve into white dots and which reflects the garden vegetation. In the WC, shower, and changing room areas, curtains are used to flexibly provide as much privacy as desired.

STRIPE HOUSE

Dare to wear stripes! A simple and minimal detail to get a unique house.

Architects | GAAGA studio for architecture
Project address | Wattstraat 8, 2316 SK, Leiden, The Netherlands
Gross floor area | 206 m²
Main materials | plaster
Completion | 2012

Stripe House is a small, mixed-use house located in Leiden, The Netherlands. It takes its name from the horizontal stripes carved into the façade. The house resides in a new urban planning area where clients can develop their own houses. Despite its limited size, the plot is not entirely built on. One quarter of the plot is reserved for a small enclosed garden, creating a soft transition from public to private space. The ground floor houses the office space and the patio, the next level contains the kitchen, living and dining space, while two bedrooms and a bathroom are located on the upper floor. The large void along the north façade is the focal point in the house. The large window at the top offers an abundance of natural light. The huge exterior walls are made tangible and appealing by means of horizontal grooves in the plaster. The grooves, with a total length of approximately 7,000 meters, are handmade and carved into a semi-hardened plaster.

Architects | Rios Clementi Hale Studios
Interior designers | Waldo's Designs
Project address | Los Angeles, CA, USA
Gross floor area | 359 m²
Main materials | limestone, glass, steel beams (concealed)
Completion | 2012

The house is a spa-like retreat for an international fashion designer. The architect's renovation features 12 meters of sliding glass opening onto spectacular views of Los Angeles and the Pacific Ocean. Created for seamless entertainment and relaxed living, the house uses a limited materials palette and simplified detailing for a sophisticated, minimal aesthetic. Rios Clementi Hale Studios also designed the landscape and outdoor spaces, including a 21-meter-long lap pool with infinity edges. The pool provides a dramatic backdrop to the home and ends with a fire table, drawing occupants to the spectacular view. The landscape is arranged as a planted bento box – an orthogonal grid containing various elements, while grasses, hedges, gravel, and a row of trees are laid in bands across the front yard creating layers of privacy.

JESSIE CHEN RLSIDENCE

Sophistication in minimalism: the combination of noble materials and sleek lines make up this spa-like designer getaway.

GARAGE
LAUNDRY
GYM
SPA
STUDY
KITCHEN
POOL
POND
GUEST
BATH
BRIDGE
ENTRY
DINING
POND
WARDROBE
LIVING
POWDER
BEDROOM
TERRACE
BATH

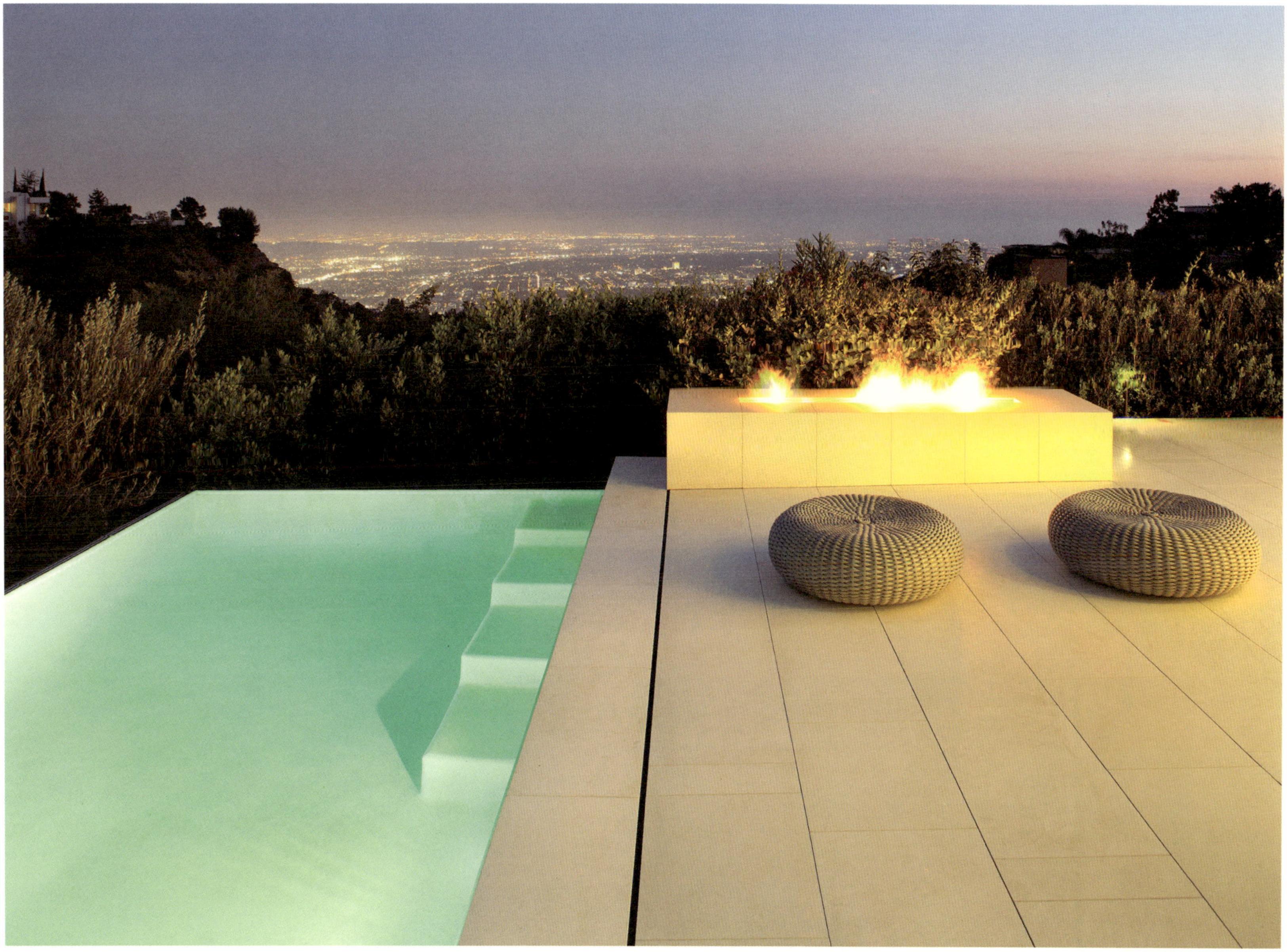

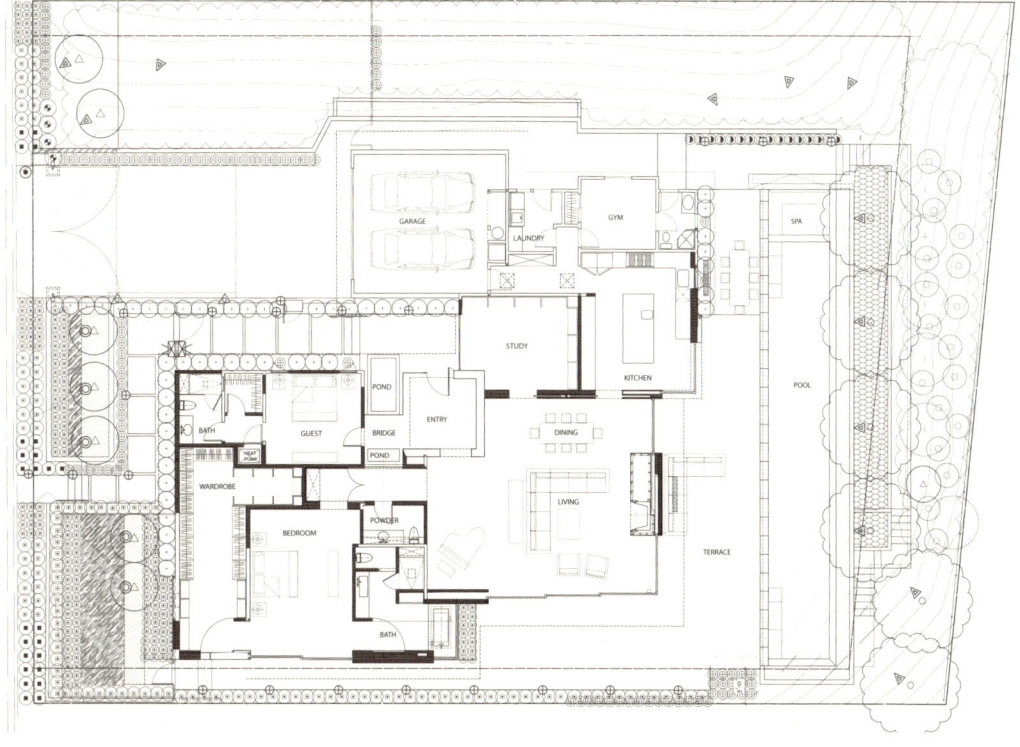

JAAX APARTMENTS

Find the odd one out in Brussels' Rue Stallaert!
A modern maverick in the landscape of orange
brick houses.

Architects | Atelier d'architecture Pierre Hebbelinck – Pierre de Wit
Project address | 4, Rue Joseph Stallaert, 1050 Brussels, Belgium
Gross floor area | 643 m²
Main materials | brick, aluminum frames, oak, concrete
Completion | 2012

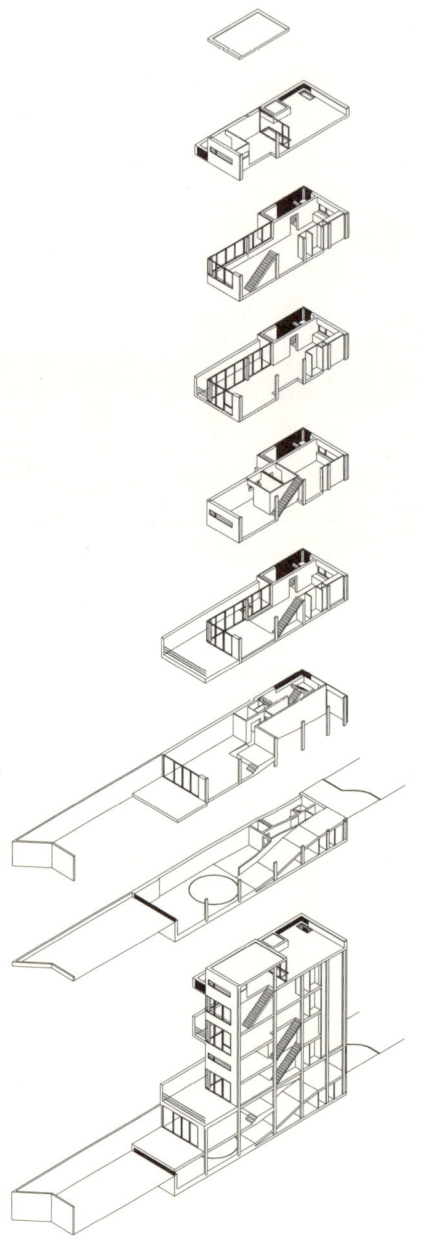

Located in the Berkendael district designed in 1902, the Rue Joseph Stallaert is one of the roads that leads to the Place Brugmann. This building is set back away from the street on the right side of the site. The program required by the client comprised the construction of a dwelling next to his home. Although the project is built on a small plot, its form is the result of various legal and urban planning constraints applicable to buildings not destined for the use of a single family. On the ground floor, a multi-use space opens out towards the garden.

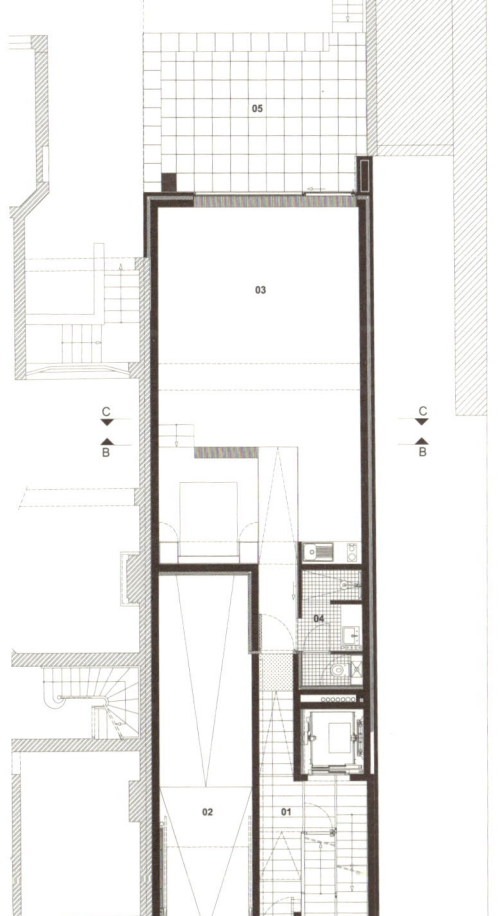

NEW FORUM ECKENBERG HIGH SCHOOL

A bright and modern face for the campus, bringing together a range of functions under one roof.

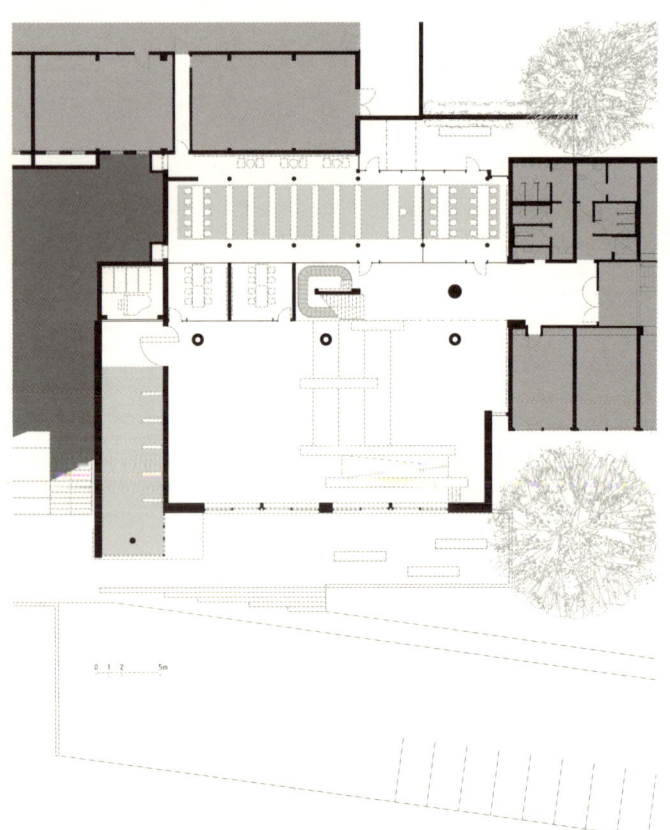

Architects | Ecker Architekten
Project address | Eckenberg 1, 74740 Adelsheim, Germany
Gross floor area | 1,125 m²
Main materials | concrete, glass, aluminum, terrazzo
Completion | 2013

The campus of the Eckenberg Academy is located on a hillside overlooking the town of Adelsheim. The first new campus building in 40 years, the Forum establishes a central campus hub, joining two existing structures on six different levels. The building is designed as a single room with multiple layers and transparent partitions. A square roof is supported by three rotationally-cast concrete columns that define the central axis of the building. The reinforced concrete roof slab is comprised of cyclical coffers, many of which integrate transparent skylights. These oculi provide natural and artificial illumination, ventilation, and sound absorption. The structure incorporates an auditorium, a library, multi-purpose rooms, a café and a student lounge. The building takes advantage of natural cross-ventilation, enabled through large operable glass louvers. Stainless steel micro-louvers integrated into the curtain wall are used for exterior sun-control.

INFINITE LANDSCAPE

Land art with meditative character. Get lost in the purity of water.

Architects | Ryo Yamada
Project address | geijyutsuno-mori minamiku Sapporo-city, Japan
Gross floor area | 7 m²
Main materials | wood
Completion | 2010

This is architecture built in a lake. But then again, if architecture is defined as something "to protect and support the human body" this is not architecture, as what this place supports is just simply the time spent here. Visitors head for the room via a 45-centimeter-wide, 14 meter-long walkway, some taking their time and walking in a straight line, others occasionally looking back to confirm the path they have taken. The room is a 1 meter-wide, 8 meter-long, 2 meter-high angled space. In the black painted interior there is only the floor into which the water has flooded. As a result, visitors can only see the "color of the water" penetrated by the light from the bed of the lake. This is a work of land art that floats above the center of a lake. But then again, if land art is defined as something that guides people, this is not land art, as where we are being led is just to the world that surrounds us all the time.

Architects | Fujiwara-Muro architects
Project address | Higashinada, Kobe-shi, Japan
Gross floor area | 63 m²
Main materials | wood
Completion | 2012

This house is located in a residential area at the heart of the city of Kobe and is flanked by houses on either side. The client's demands were typical for a family of four – a parking space, a bright living room, two rooms for the children, and a bedroom. A characteristic feature of the house is its rooftop space. The rooftop can be reached by climbing through a hatch accessible from the loft above the bedroom. A unique element of the house is the red cedar wood fixed to the exterior façade. Due to fire prevention regulations in the region, only incombustible materials can be used for construction.

HOUSE IN NADA

Small but not cramped. The embodiment of Japanese know-how about creating space in spite of the most challenging restrictions.

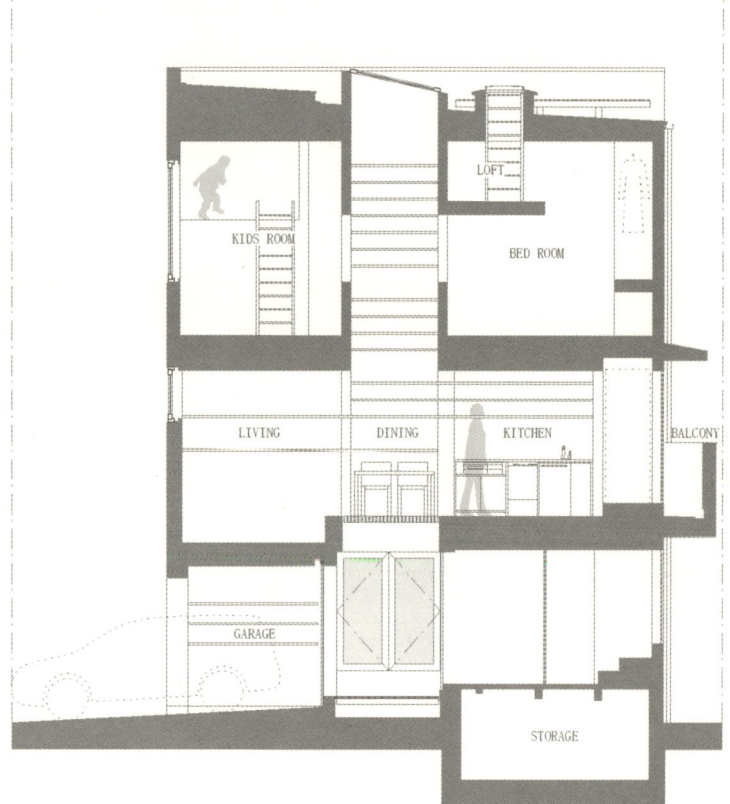

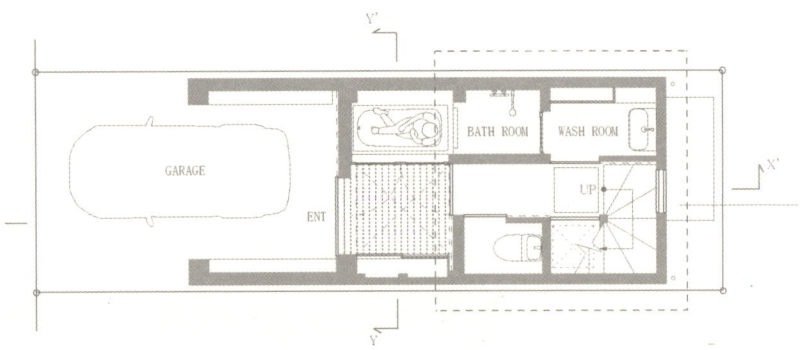

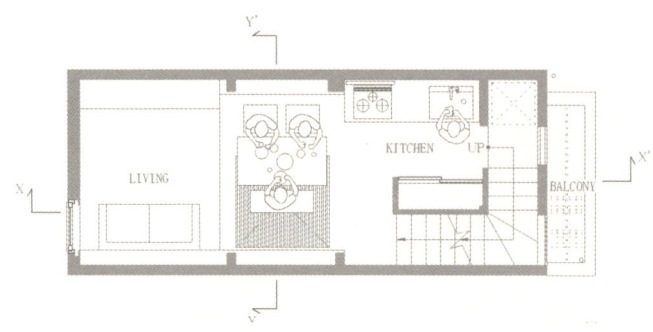

KIDS ROOM
VOID
BED ROOM
CL
CL
KIDS ROOM

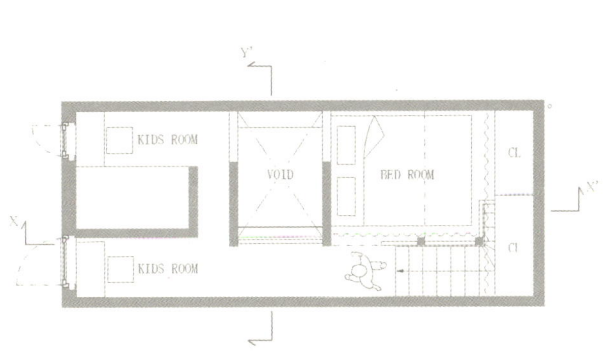

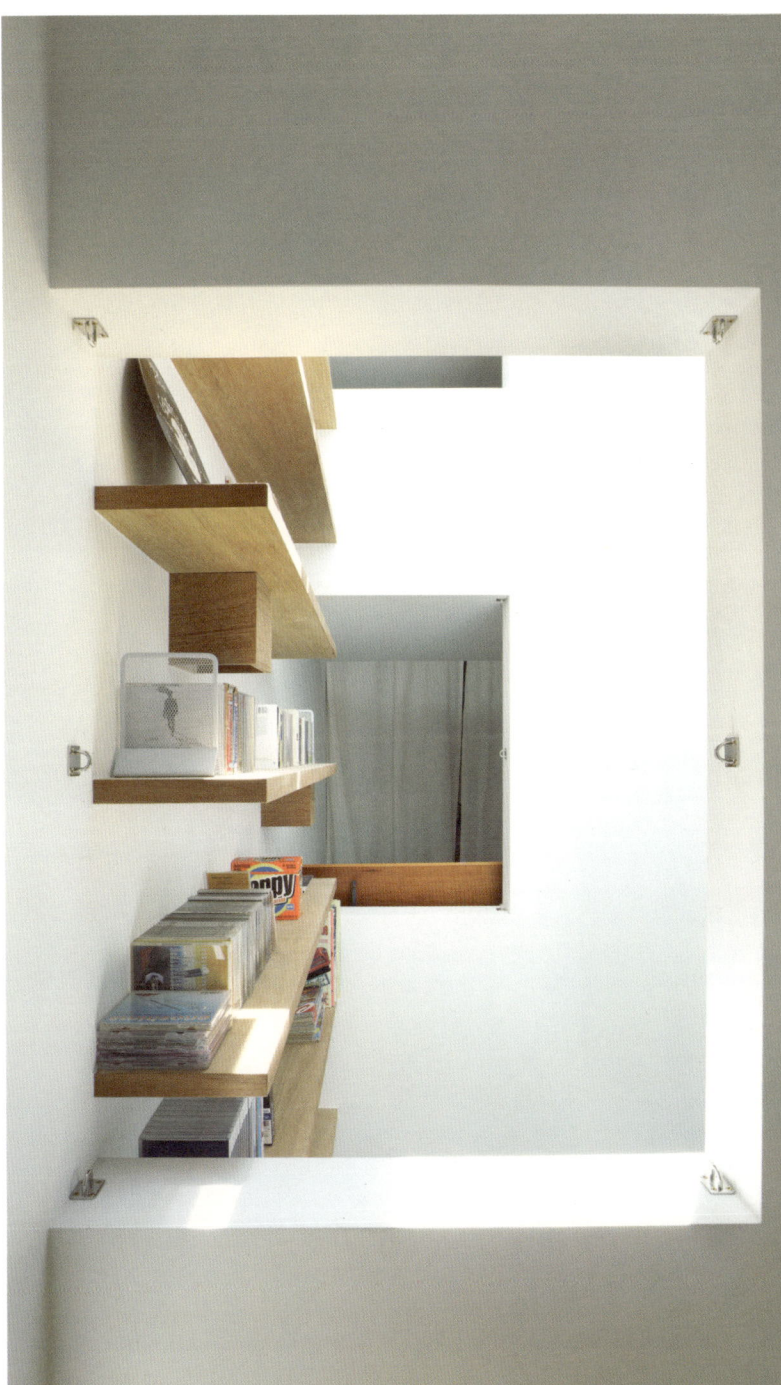

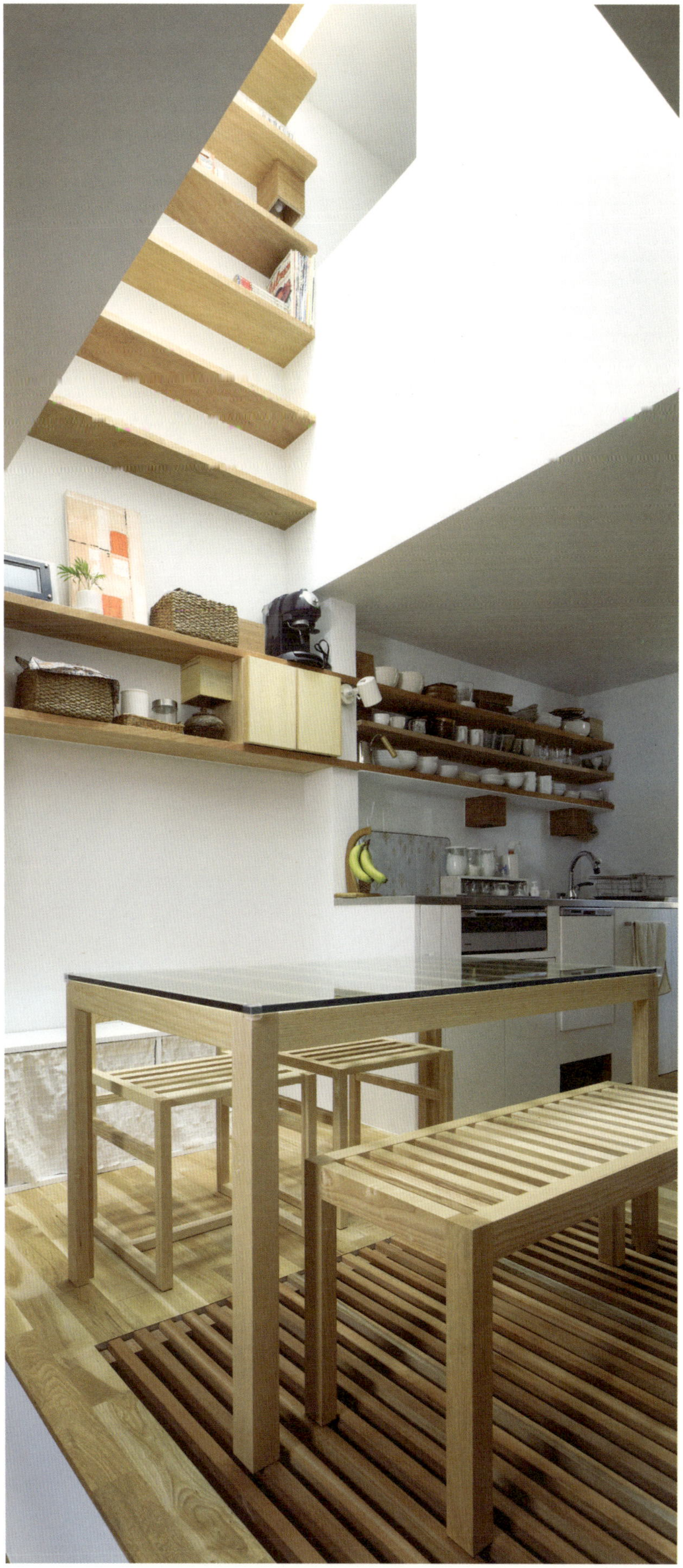

Architect | Henri Cleinge
Project address | 165, 167 Avenue Beaumont, H2S 1J2 Montreal, Canada
Gross floor area | 300 m²
Main materials | concrete, corten steel, cedar wood, American walnut
Completion | 2011

This urban project is located in a mixed-use area housing light industrial and residential buildings. The site is divided to accommodate the modulation of square spaces. Each space in each square module contains its own individual character and its own unique program. The central living room is a key focus of the project, located between the two concrete volumes. The materials used are exploited to define space and light. Both hard and 'soft' materials characterize the exterior; concrete and corten steel versus Sipo wood windows. Inside, concrete walls and floors contrast walnut cabinetry and cedar ceilings.

THE BEAUMONT HOUSE

Concrete versus wood, raw versus finished material.
The art of uniting opposites.

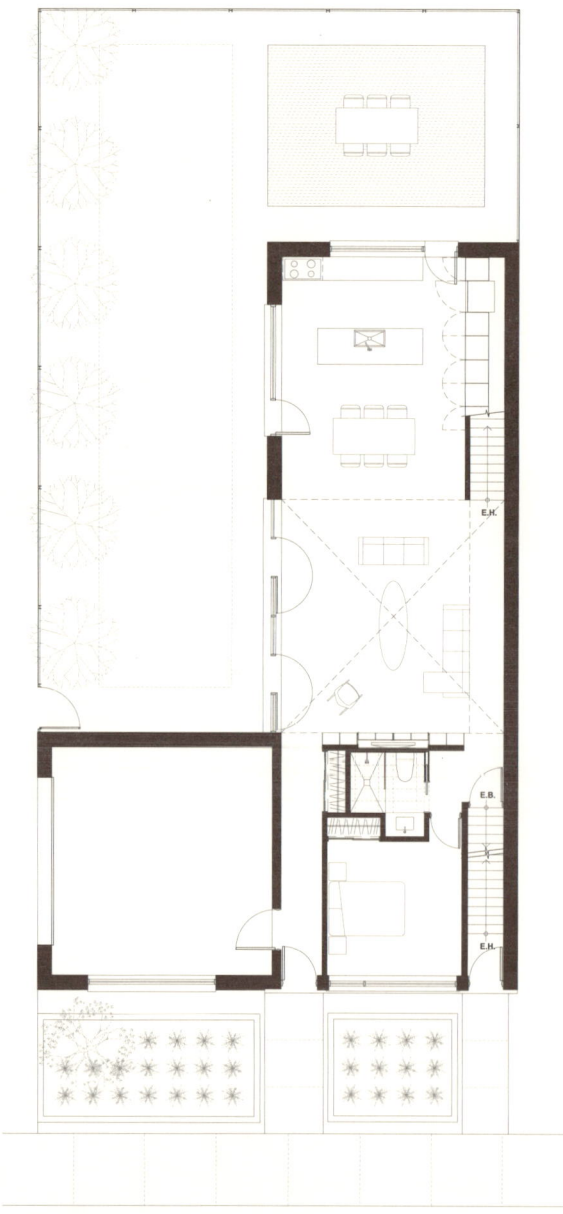

HOUSE 11x11

Living in a sculpture. An all-over cladding of wood lamella gives the house its iconic character.

The idea behind House 11x11 was to design an apparently compact house of homogeneous materials, with a low external surface but the largest possible usable area. House 11x11 is an icon for its residents, symbolic and built with a new construction method: the exterior walls and the wooden roof made of prefabricated elements are covered with a façade of wood lamella without contour battens converging on the on the roof ridge. The result is a pronounced dynamic character, reinforced by the variable density and very precise positioning of the lamella, including the integration of the wooden window frames.

Architects | Titus Bernhard Architekten
Project address | Upper Bavaria, Germany
Gross floor area | 182 m²
Main materials | wood, concrete
Completion | 2011

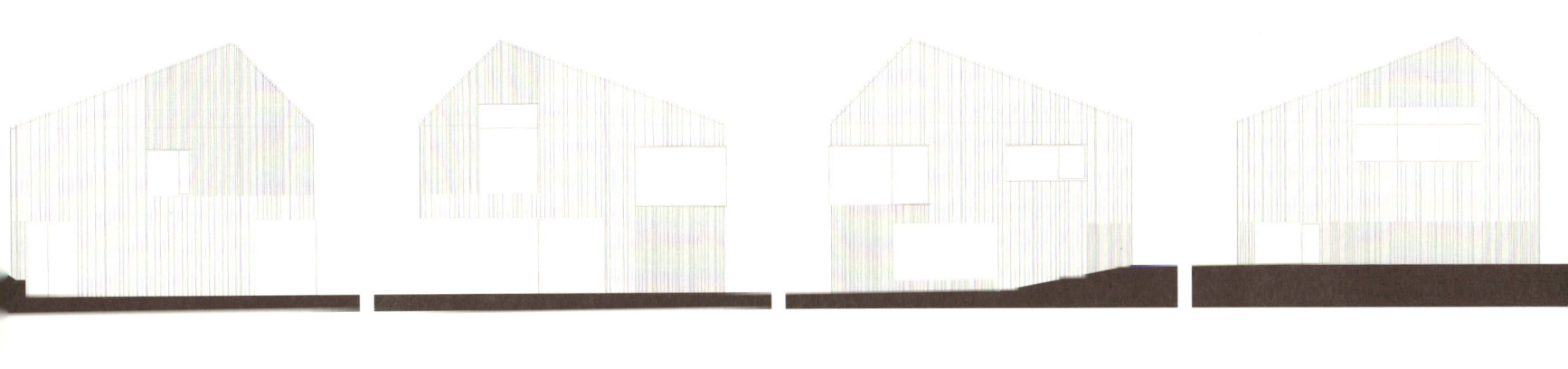

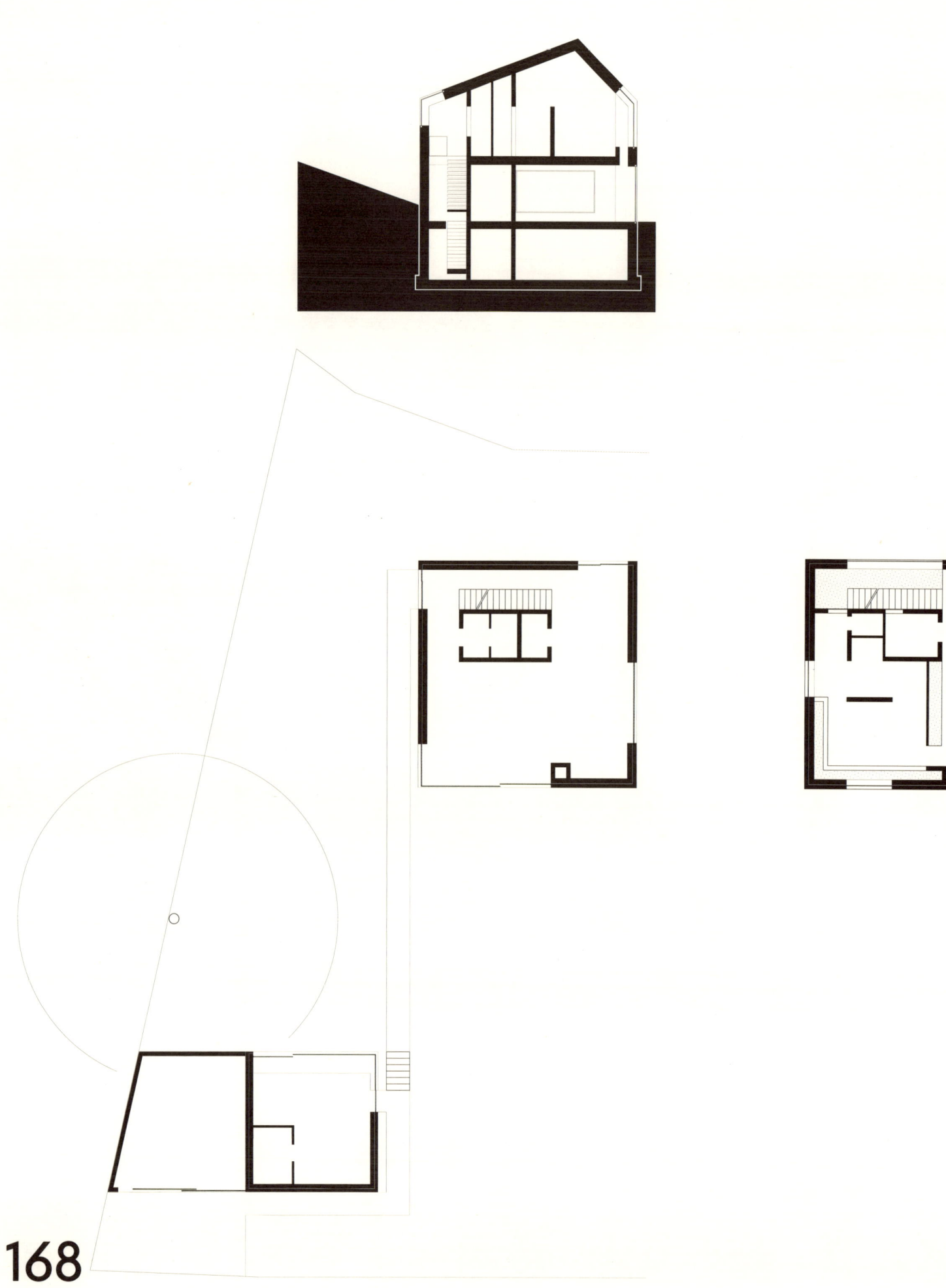

Architects | LGA Architectural Partners
Project address | 156 Galloway Road, Toronto, Ontario, Canada M1E 1X2
Gross floor area | 929 m²
Main materials | wood, steel
Completion | 2011

The Scarborough Child and Family Life Centre in eastern Toronto is designed to reflect Aboriginal culture and community. The center grew from close collaboration between LGA Architectural Partners, staff from the Native Child and Family Services of Toronto, Elders and the local Aboriginal community. Native culture is expressed through abstract forms and through local and natural materials. From the street, the building presents a shell of rusted corten steel that folds from the roof to become punctuated by bay windows and skylights. Its 'underside', facing a playground and wood lot, has a softer appearance, clad in local eastern white cedar with a timber roof and canopy that visually merges with the wood of the building's interior. Reflecting Aboriginal cultural philosophies about environmental stewardship and benefiting future generations, the building is designed with high environmental standards.

SCARBOROUGH CHILD AND FAMILY LIFE CENTRE

Expressing Native culture through abstract forms, local materials and a deep environmental consciousness.

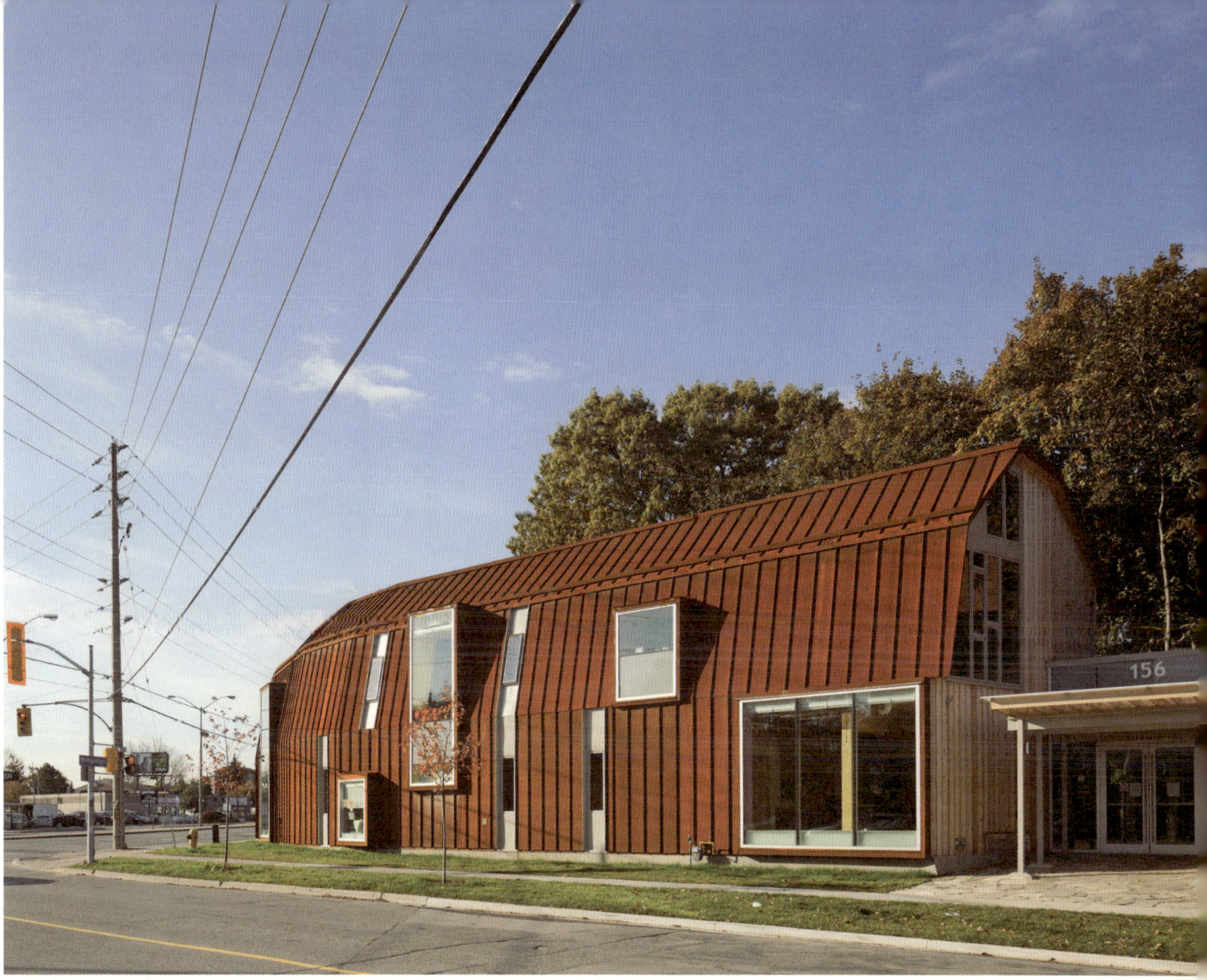
156

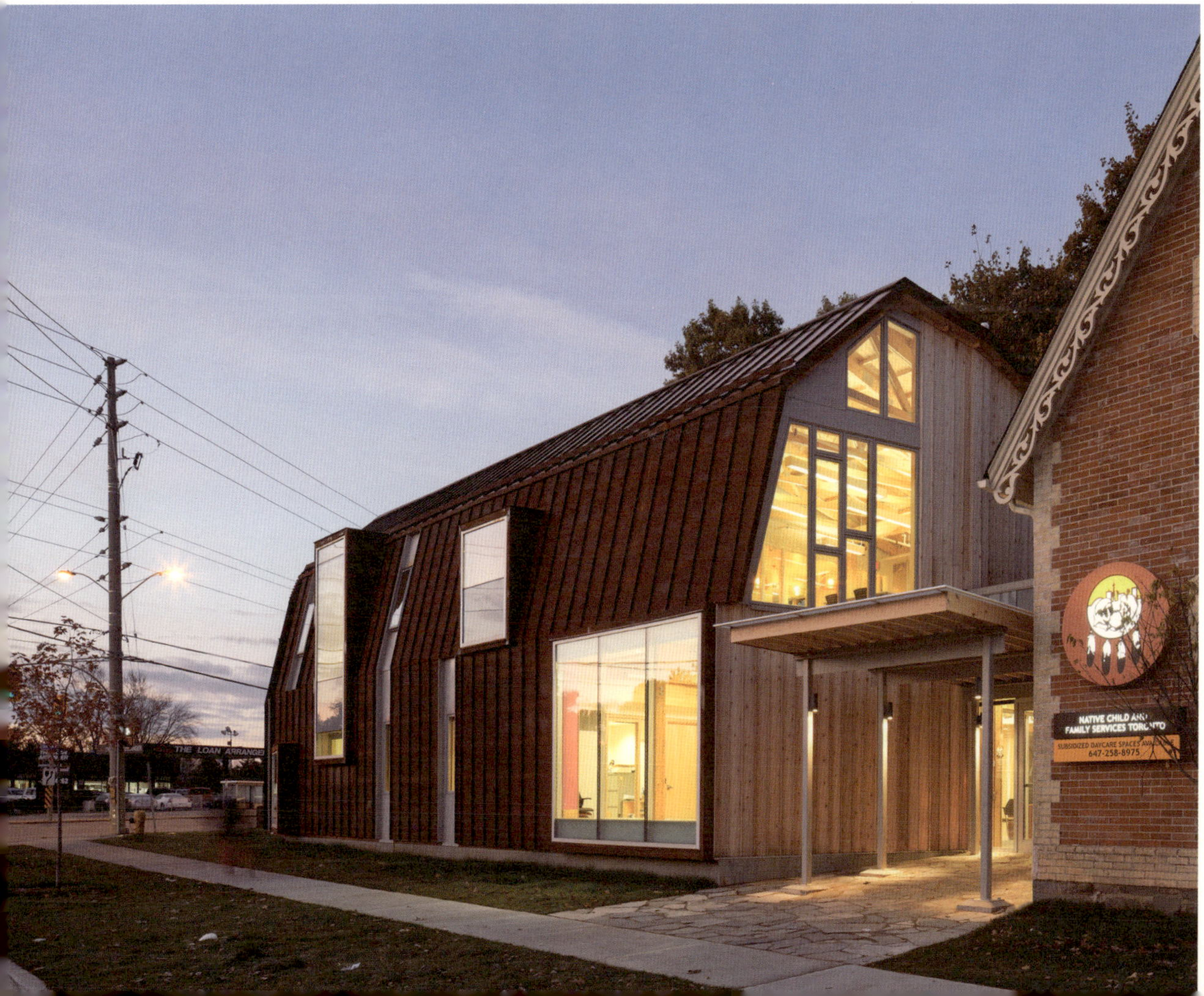
NATIVE CHILD AND
FAMILY SERVICES TORONTO
647-258-8975

ST. MARTIN'S CHURCH COMMUNITY CENTER

Just a small intervention, not imposing, but nevertheless a good deed.

This project involved remodeling the rectory and community center, as well as the connection to St. Martin's Church. In addition to the usual demands that come with such a project – renewal, functional improvements and an energy upgrade – the architects also paid close attention to careful detailing and established a greater spatial elegance with the glazed walkway. The urban appearance of this sensitive area as a whole has been improved. The work undertaken on the original building is an exemplary enhancement of both the church and the urban context.

Architects | KM Architekten
Project address | Martinsplatz 5, 34117, Kassel, Germany
Gross floor area | 715 m²
Main materials | glass
Completion | 2012

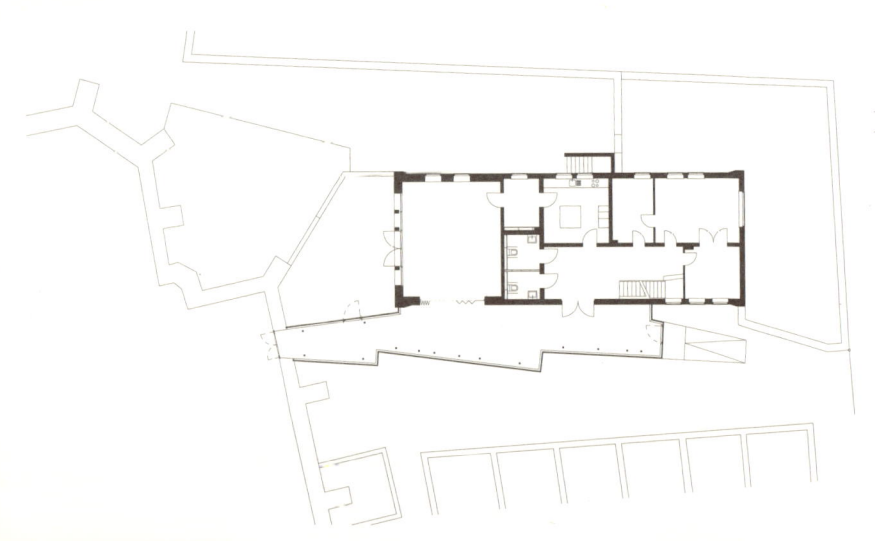

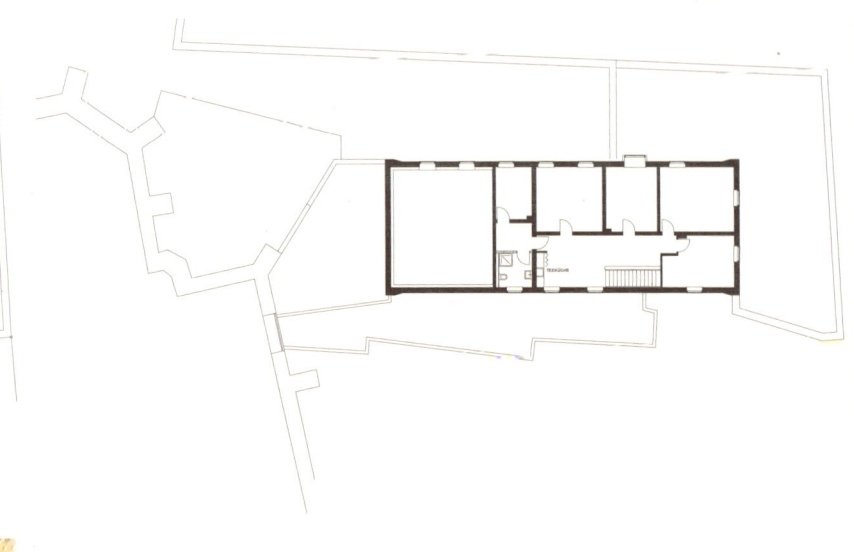

178

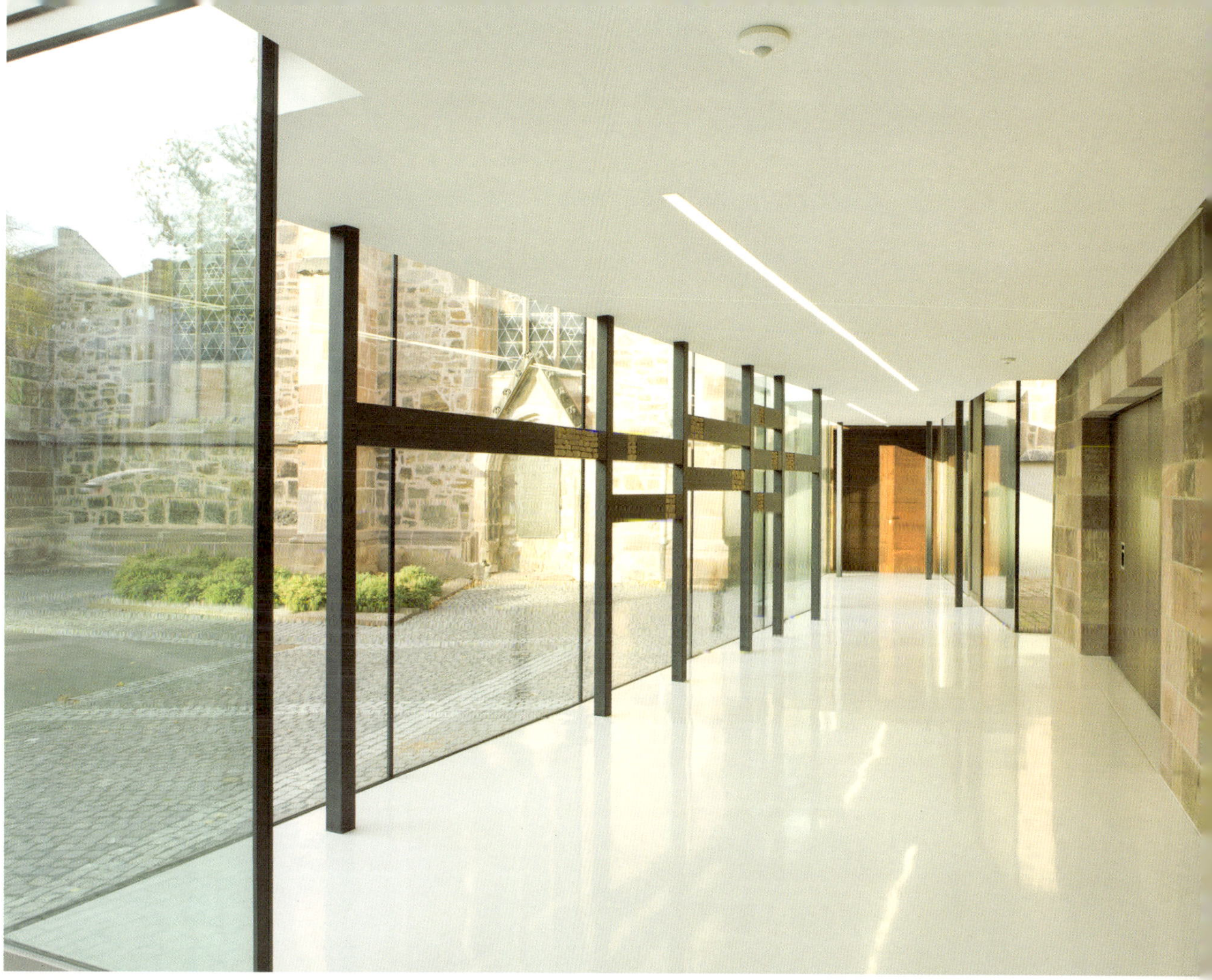

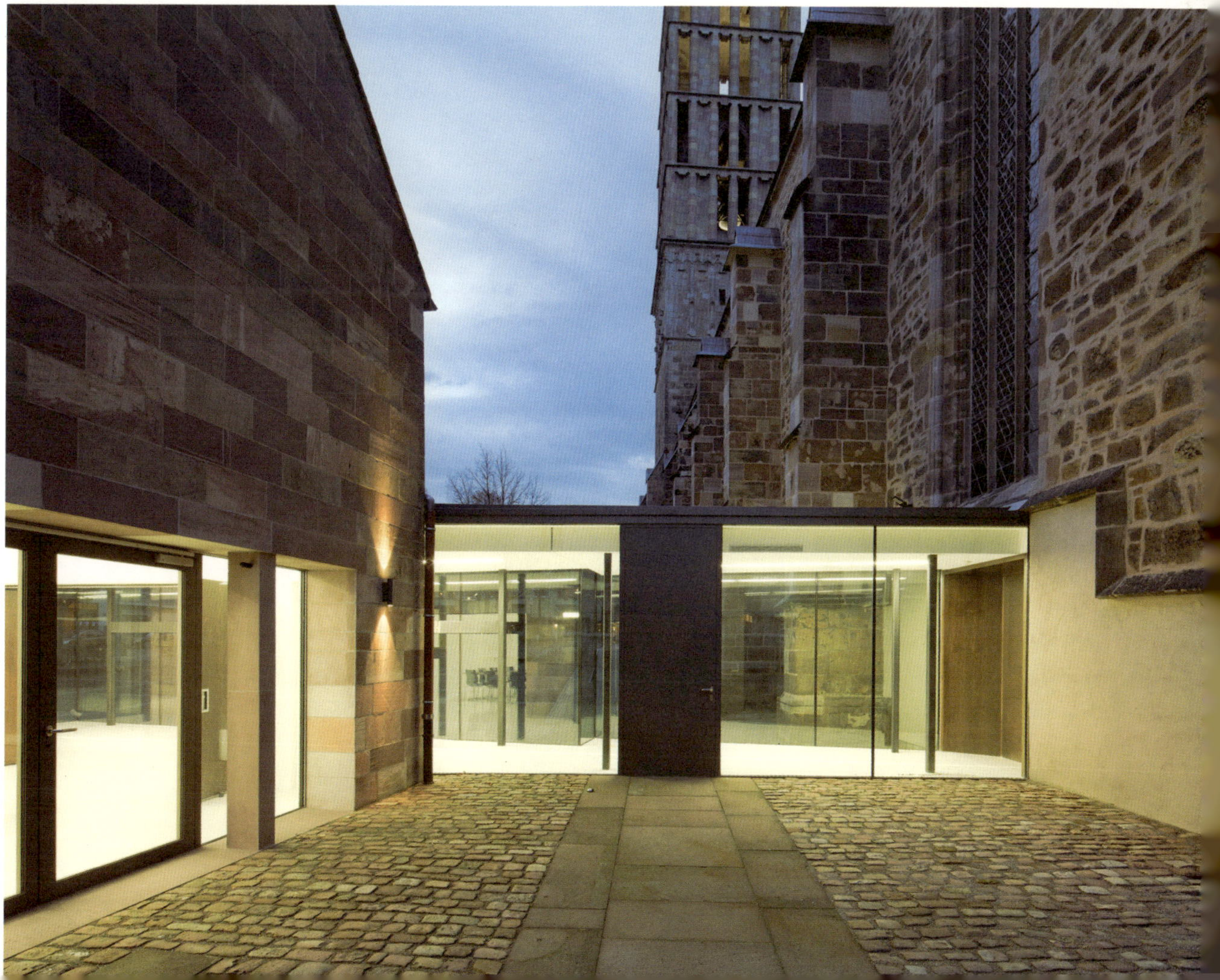

The Sackler Building provides purpose-built accommodation for painting students at the Royal College of Art, allowing them to work together under one roof for the first time in over ten years. The brief was to create contemporary purpose built studios to match the quality and character of the very best traditional painting studios in London. The building was always conceived as a conversion: the old building has been transformed into a series of new day-lit spaces under a new roof form through the insertion of an independent steel structure within the existing brick enclosure. This significantly increased the usable height of the building, providing six double-height, top-lit studio spaces arranged in series off a wide central corridor space. A galleried mezzanine floor overlooks the double-height studios, providing access to an upper level of smaller top-lit studios.

180

THE SACKLER BUILDING

Give the old-fashioned bricks a fresh look with
a brand new silver top hat.

Architects | Haworth Tompkins
Project address | 14 Howie Street, London SW11 4AY, United Kingdom
Gross floor area | 1,280 m²
Main materials | anodized aluminum, galvanized steel, existing brick, concrete, oak wood
Completion | 2009

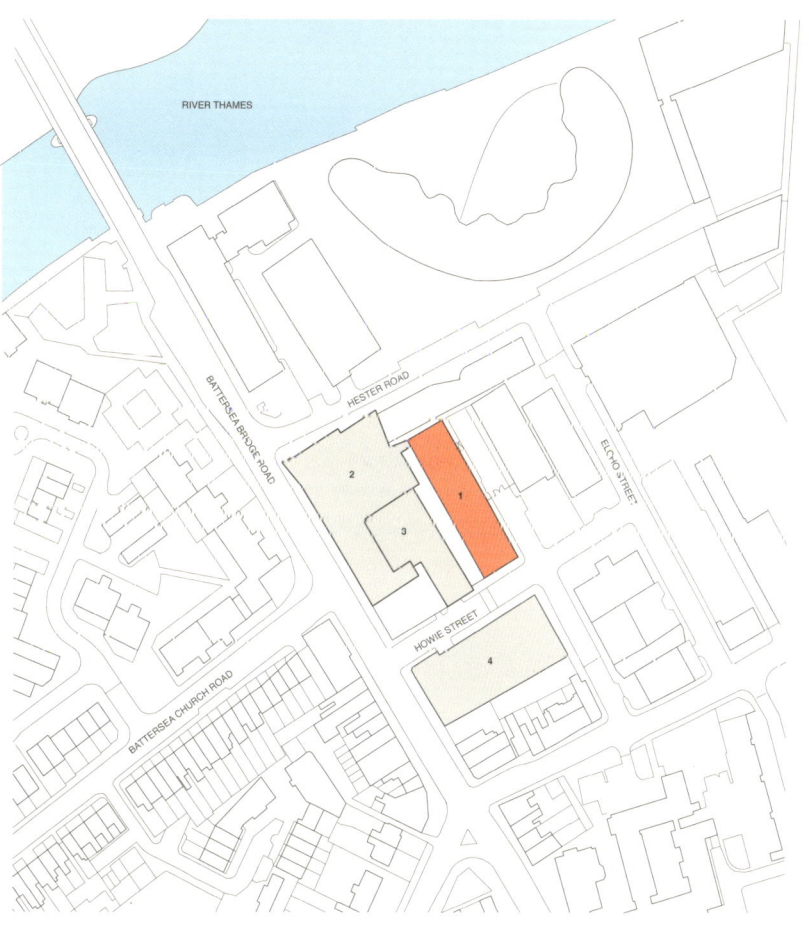

ROYAL COLLEGE OF ART
BATTERSEA

1   PHASE 1: SACKLER BUILDING
      PAINTING SCHOOL

2   PHASE 2: DYSON BUILDING
      PRINTMAKING AND PHOTOGRAPHY
      INNOVATION RCA

3   PHASE 3: WOO BUILDING
      CERAMICS & GLASS AND GSM&J

4   SCULPTURE SCHOOL

A GLASS BOX FOR VIEWING THE ORCHARD

Back to basics: Only corrugated iron and glass separate the desks from this Garden of Eden. But please, don't break the charm; don't eat the apples!

Architects | Branch Studio Architects
Project address | Bellevue Orchard, Officer, Victoria, Australia
Gross floor area | 25 m²
Main materials | recycled corrugated iron, glass, plywood
Completion | 2012

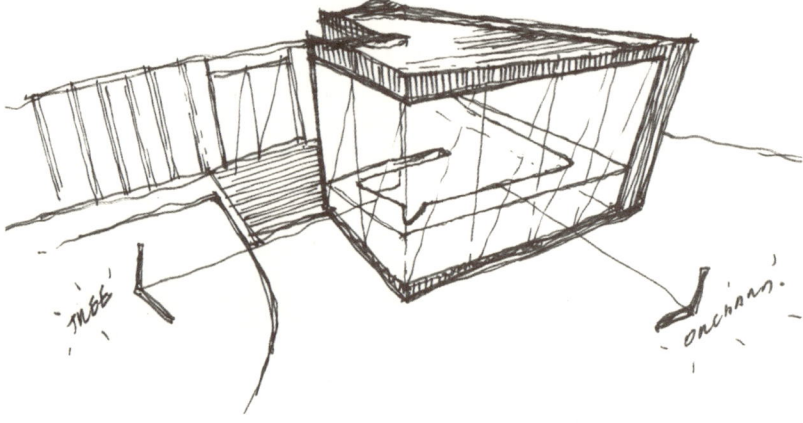

A small studio space is designed to accommodate two architects, a landscape architect and a meeting area. The form of the building was composed to maximize views and functionally accommodate the required program. The architects' workspaces are arranged to provide views of the orchard, while the landscape architect faces directly into a small landscaped courtyard. The solid façades help to block views of the car park and nearby sheds. The recycled corrugated iron was collected from paddocks surrounding the site and used as a façade material to contrast the large glazed areas. Inside, raw plywood floors and ceilings contrast the white walls. All joinery is custom-designed, laser-cut layered plywood with burnt black expressed edges. A series of layered plywood boxes are 'tucked' into wall cavities and form spaces for book and folder storage.

INTENSIVE

MINI

INGENIOUS

ICO

NIC

INSPIRING

INCOMPARABLE

WEINKULTURGUT LONGEN-SCHLÖDER

Holiday in the vineyard. Take a seat in the garden of your little stone cottage and enjoy a powerful Riesling... Cheers!

This 6,500-square-meter, family-owned property offers its guests the chance to re-connect with nature. Italian architect Matteo Thun, well known for his holistic and sustainable approach to architecture and interior design, has supported the family's project with integral planning and implementation. Nestled into the orchard, the new vineyard houses convey the philosophy of the Longen family. Surrounded by fruit and walnut, lime and chestnut trees, Longen's guests live in small houses built with local stone. Each of the 20 houses has access to a small wooden terrace and a private garden. The design of the 20-square-meter slate houses is pure, bright and clear. Lots of wood, plenty of white, original fabrics and natural materials determine the interior's composition. The project has been awarded the Architecture prize for wine 2013.

Architects | Matteo Thun & Partners
Landscape architect | Johannes Cox
Local architects | Stein-Hemmes-Wirtz
Project address | Kirchenweg 9, 54340 Longuich, Germany
Gross floor area | 900 m²
Main materials | slate, wood
Completion | 2012

WINZERHAUS-LONGEN

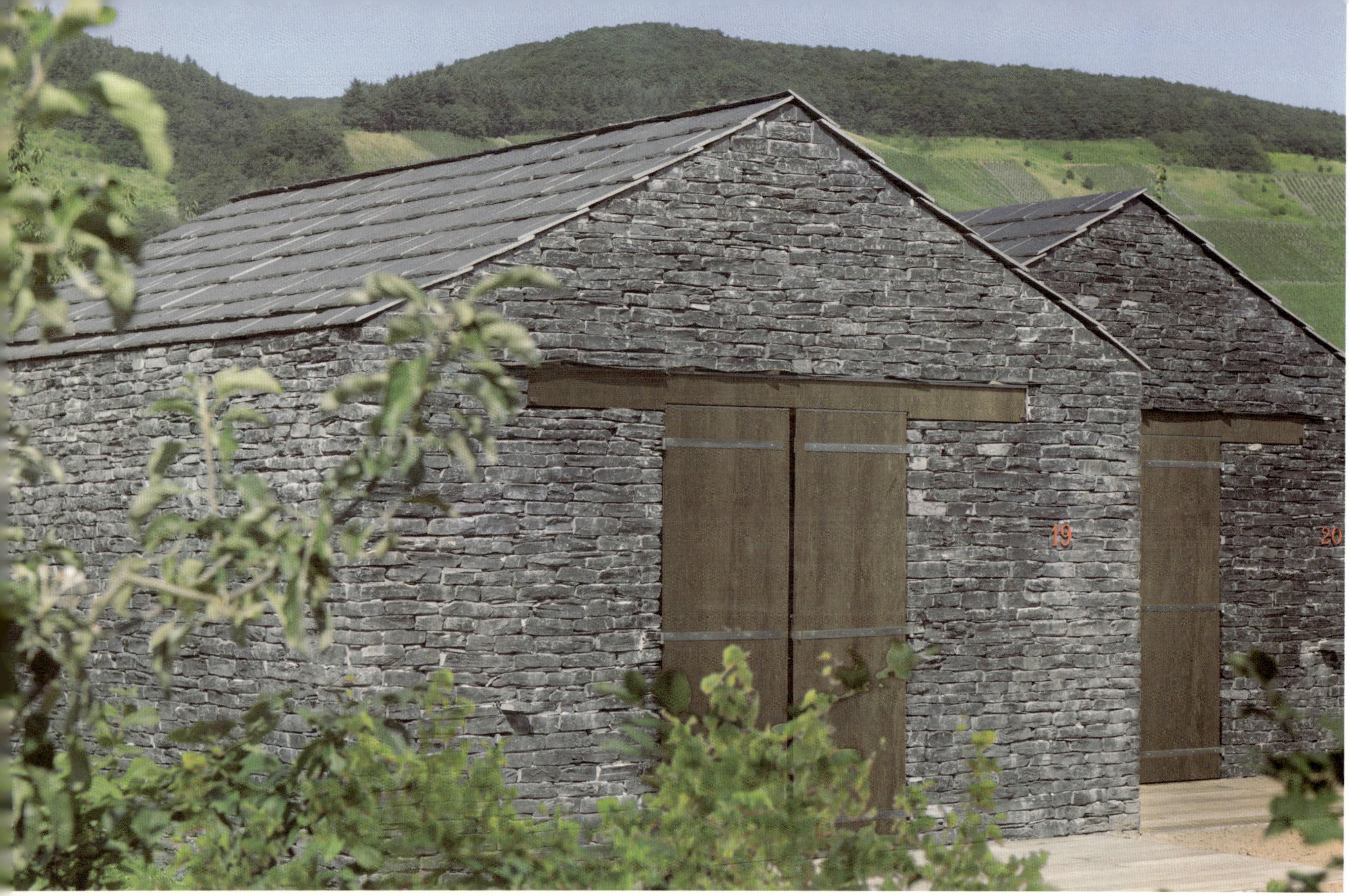
19

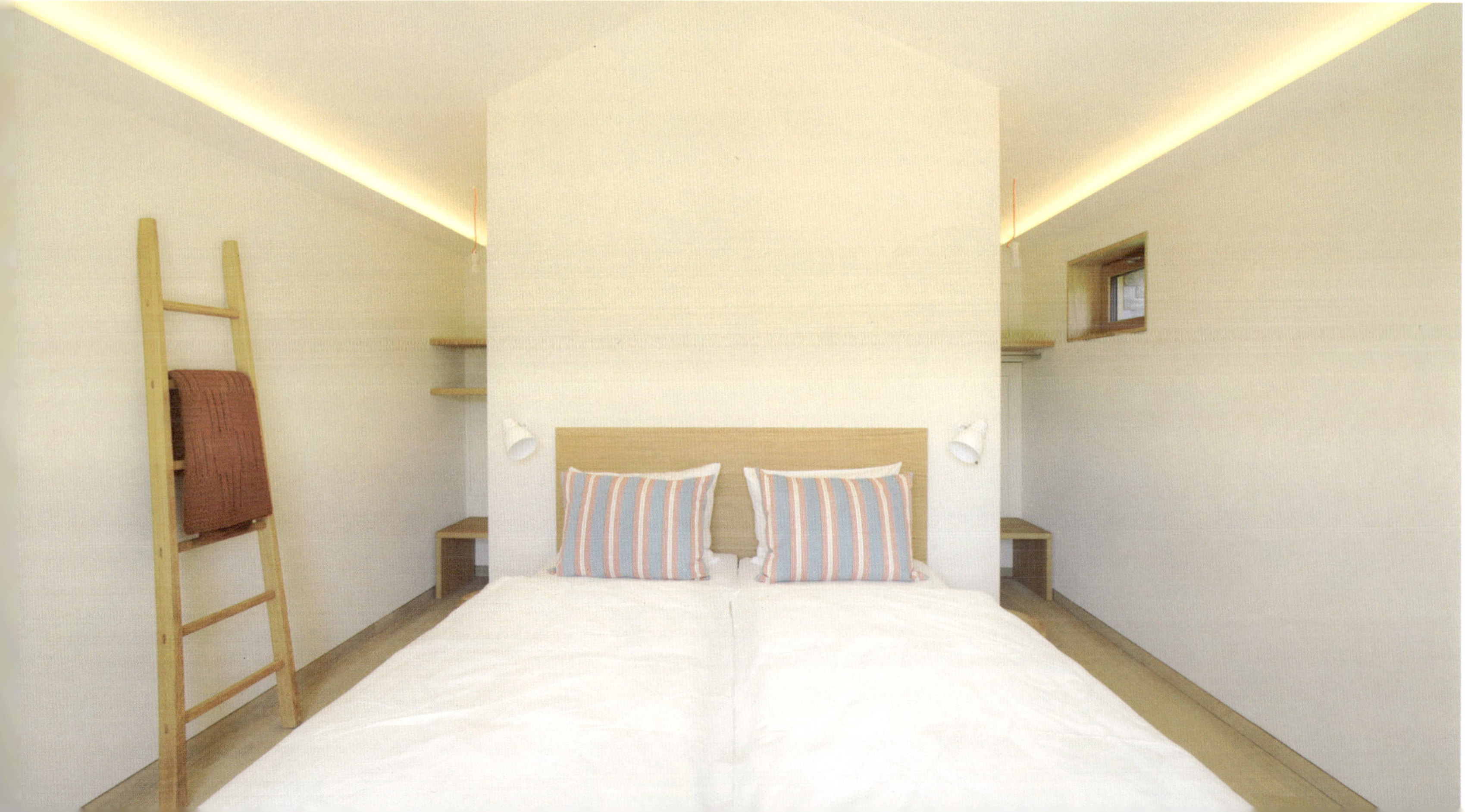

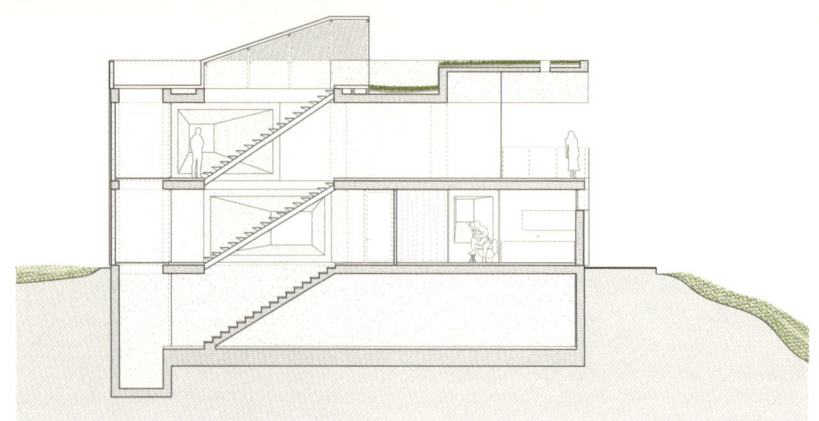

This house is located in an unspoilt border area between Africa and Europe with a wealth of scenic and cultural heritage. The house is organized in four areas with different programs. All are connected visually and spatially by the main vertical communication element of the house; the staircase. The bedrooms, laundry and main entrance are all located on the ground floor, while the living area, kitchen, dining room, bathroom are all located on the upper floor. The design frames and makes the most of views across the landscape.

196

WINDSURFER HOUSE

A house starring nature. Framing the views of
the ocean and shaped for watching the waves.
Be ready for a ride!

Architects | Javier Peña Galiano
Project address | Puntas de Calnegre, 30876 Lorca, Spain
Gross floor area | 612 m²
Main materials | concrete, ceramic thermal blocks
Completion | 2011

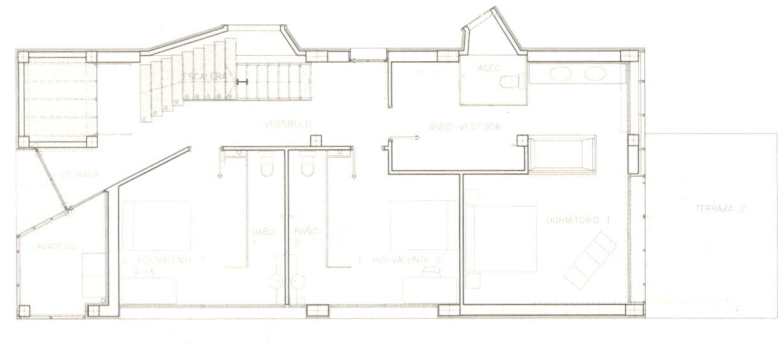

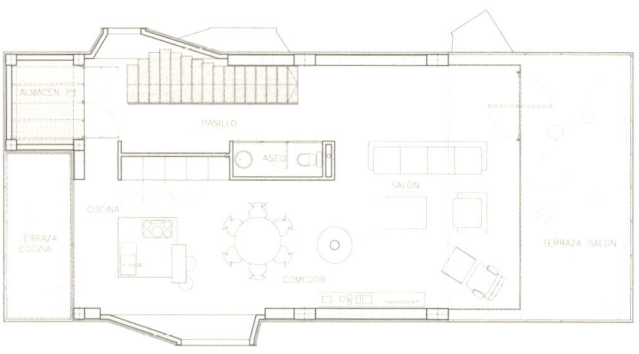

198

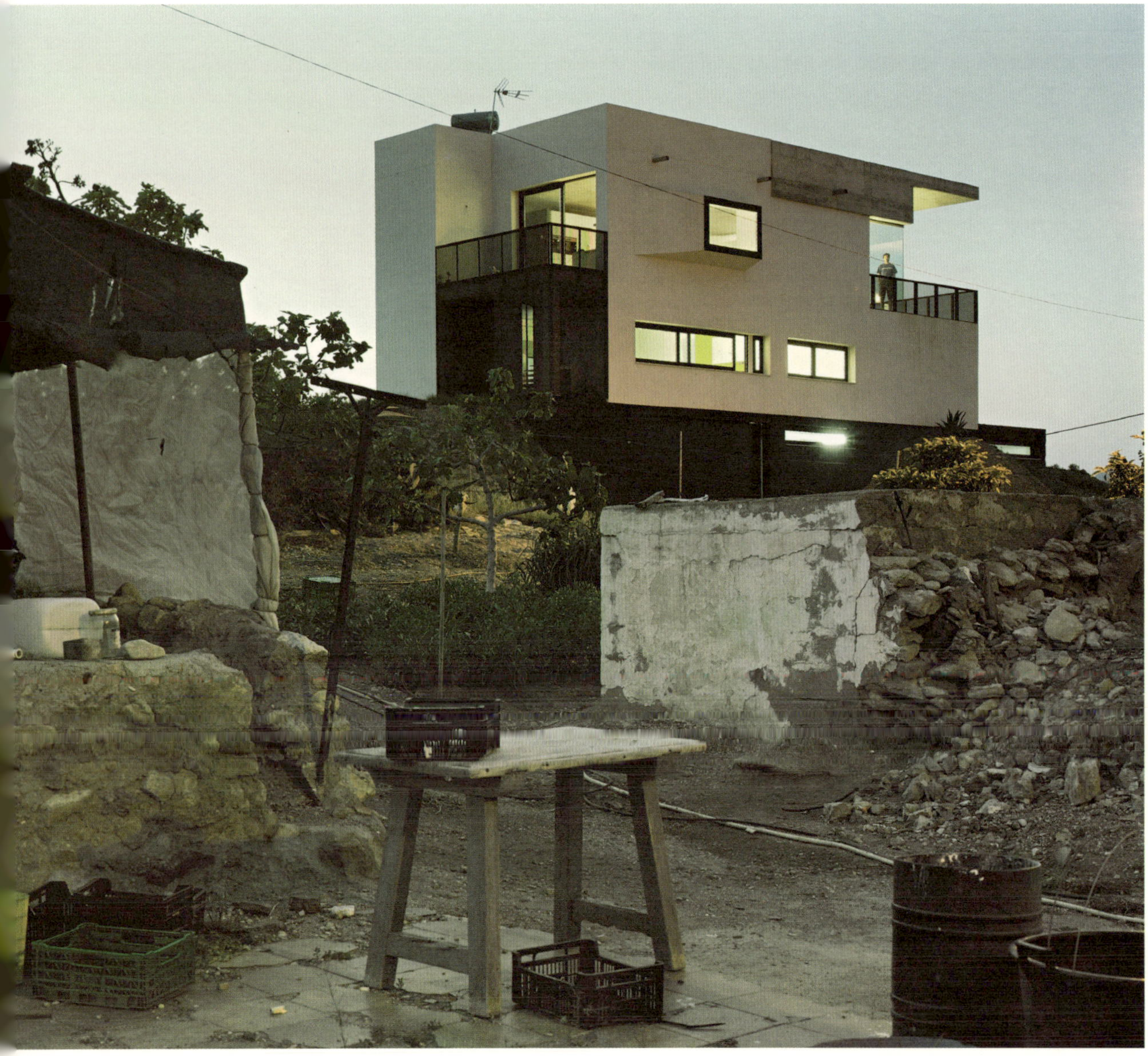

This design comprises a reinforced steel bridge construction. The upper level is a box girder structure, resting on two lateral abutments. This arrangement permits the development of an open-plan ground floor that is extremely flexible and thus ideal for exhibiting the company's own glass interior products. The building presents a very open and transparent ground floor, which contrasts the introverted office area on the upper floor. Two landscaped courtyards help to structure the administration areas. The entire concrete core is encased in a façade of suspended isolation glass, which reflects not only the company's innovative nature, but also hints at the kind of wares one can inspect inside. In terms of the sparse material selection, only the soft noise protection felt lamella, and the furnishings of black MDF offer an optical contrast. Outside, a graveled area and a line of trees shield the building from the street.

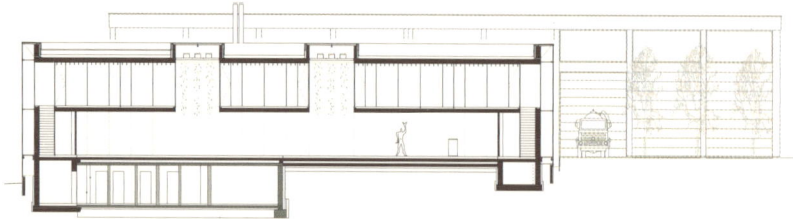

GLASS COMPETENCE CENTER

Smooth and hard, light and heavy, transparent and reflecting, material and immaterial. Explore the unexpected characteristics of glass.

Architects | becker architekten
Project address | Im Allmey 14, 87435 Kempten, Germany
Gross floor area | 873 m²
Main materials | glass, concrete, planting
Completion | 2008

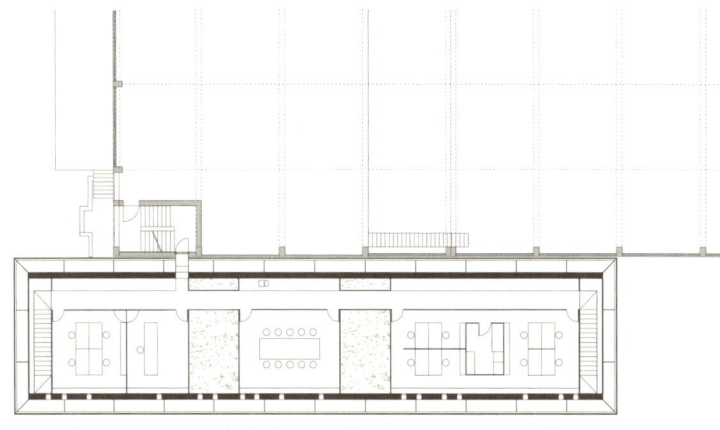

This new seminar building in Gut Siggen respects the architectural ensemble, which
is characterized by the historical building and the open space at its center. Within
the original building sequence, the single-story adopts to the location and orientation of the former horse stable. The pavilion-like building does not intrude upon
the surroundings and preserves the symmetry of the building complex, leaving the
manor house as an independent building. The use of natural and modern materials,
such as wood, concrete and steel, giving the new building its independent character.
The building is raised slightly above the lawn, which has the effect of emphasizing
its lightweight appearance. While the seminar areas and foyer open out towards the
central space, the private and independent guest rooms are oriented towards the
outside and nature.

SEMINAR BUILDING GUT SIGGEN

A light pavilion floating over the meadow, gentle and modest. Nothing disturbs the rustic charm of this historical ensemble.

Architects | Auer+Weber+Assoziierte
Project address | Gut Siggen, 23777 Heringsdorf, Germany
Gross floor area | 715 m²
Main materials | steel, wood, concrete
Completion | 2007

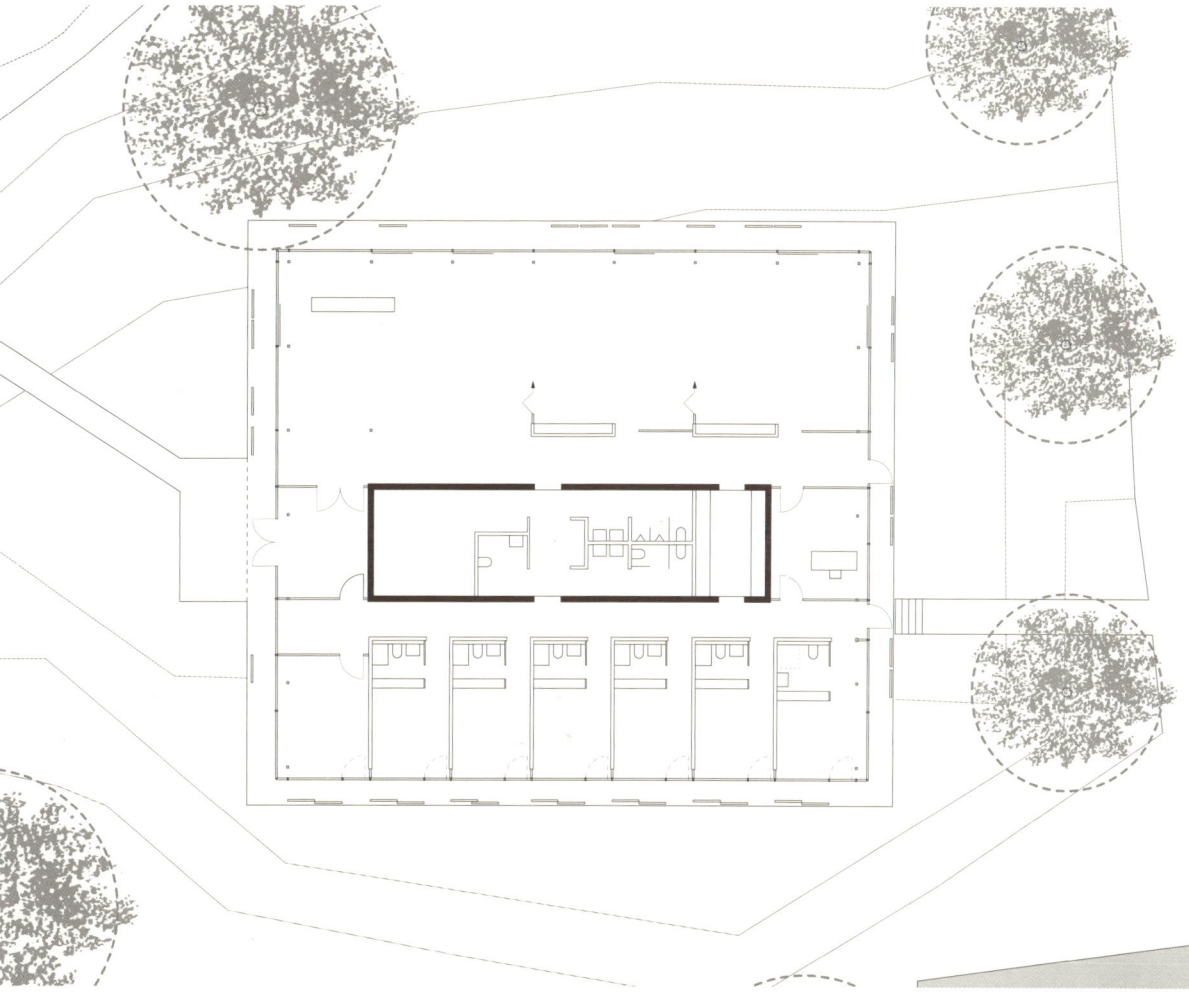

MIDDLE SCHOOL IN VOUVRY

What a panorama! And the view of this golden bar
in the pasturelands along the Rhone River is no
less spectacular.

Architects | Berrel Berrel Kräutler
Project address | Avenue de la Gare 31,
 1896 Vouvry, Switzerland
Gross floor area | 9,400 m²
Main materials | copper, brass
Completion | 2013

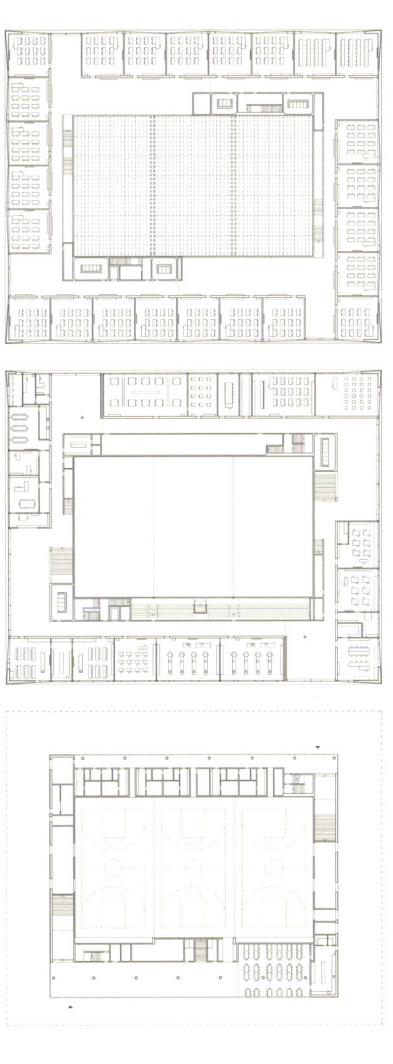

The spectacular topography of the Swiss Alps is reflected in the project by the connection between the school building and gymnasium. The gymnasium forms the core of the new school complex. Illuminated from above, it is surrounded by the classrooms on the two upper floors. On the ground floor, the building volume is drawn back behind the building line, creating a continuous roofed space that characterizes the 'floating' character of the building. A large flight of stairs provides access to the upper levels. Uninterrupted views through the building link what is happening in the gymnasium with activity in other parts of the complex.

213

Architects | Stéphane Bigoni + Antoine Mortemard
Project address | Quai de Boisguilbert, 76000 Rouen, France
Gross floor area | 1,800 m²
Main materials | concrete, brick, steel, glass
Completion | 2010

Located in the historical harbor area, this project focuses on the extension of an old storage hangar between the railroad tracks and the Seine River, allowing it to house an auditorium and exhibit spaces. In the middle of the building, a large mashrabiya captures and diffracts light. At night, the lattice becomes a lantern, emerging from the floor beneath the hangar's frame. The auditorium sits partially beneath the old hangar, a concrete structure independent of the existing building frame. However, the design has a surprising twist: The back wall of the stage can be opened, incorporating views of the harbor into the design. The project won the Architecture and Urbanism Grand Prize of Haute-Normandie 2012.

CONVENTION CENTER

Attention please. Pure light and straight lines form the basis of this elegant design.

214

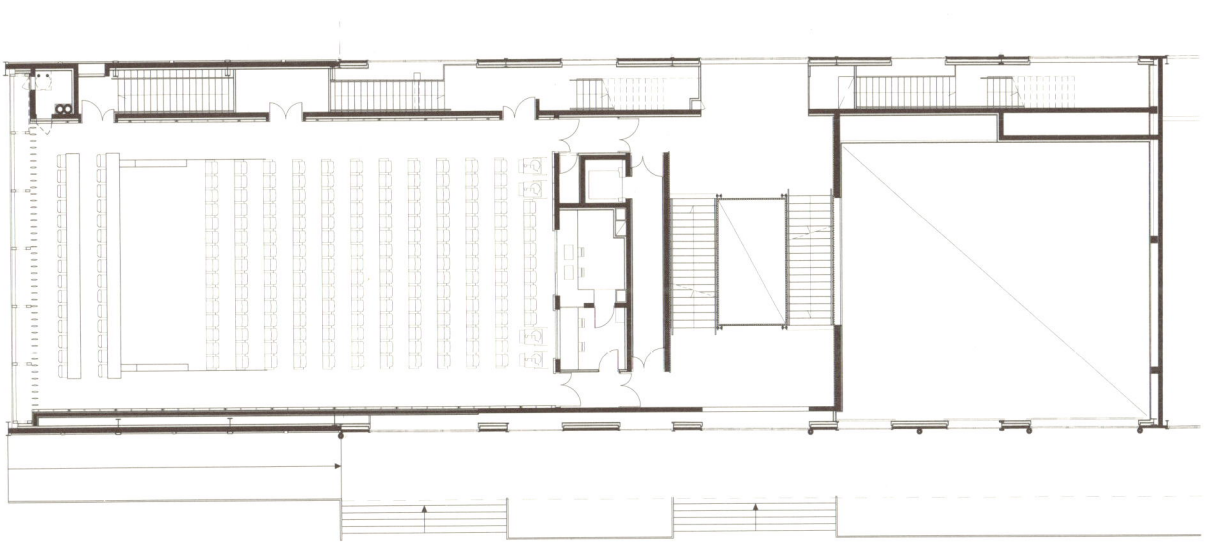

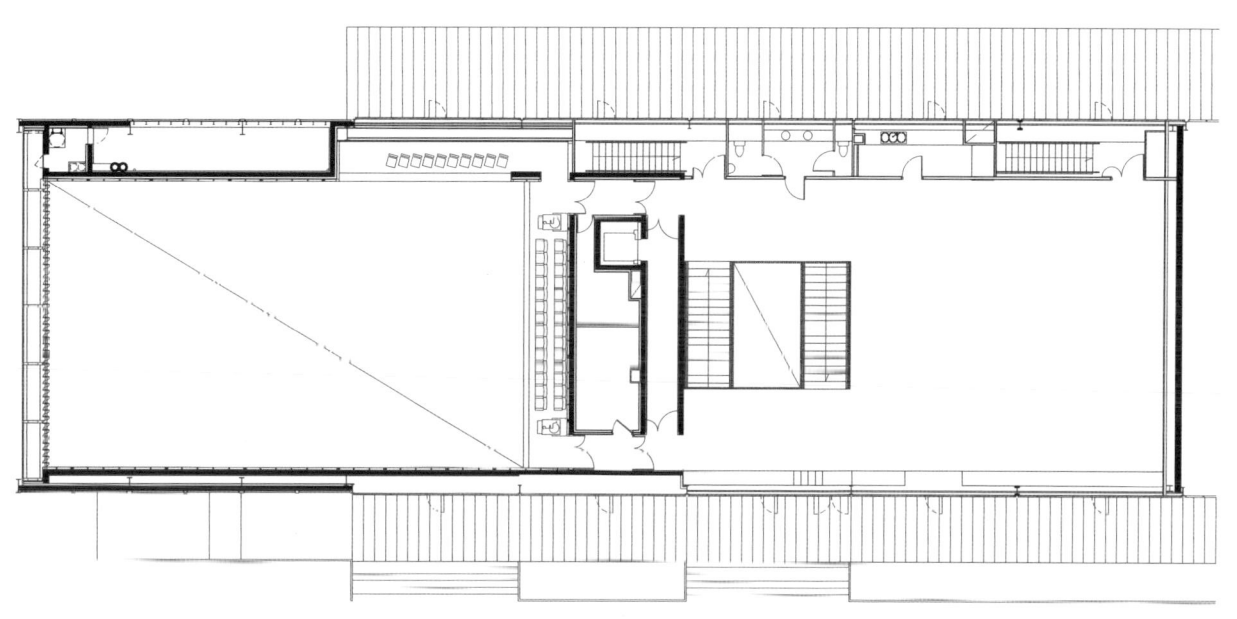

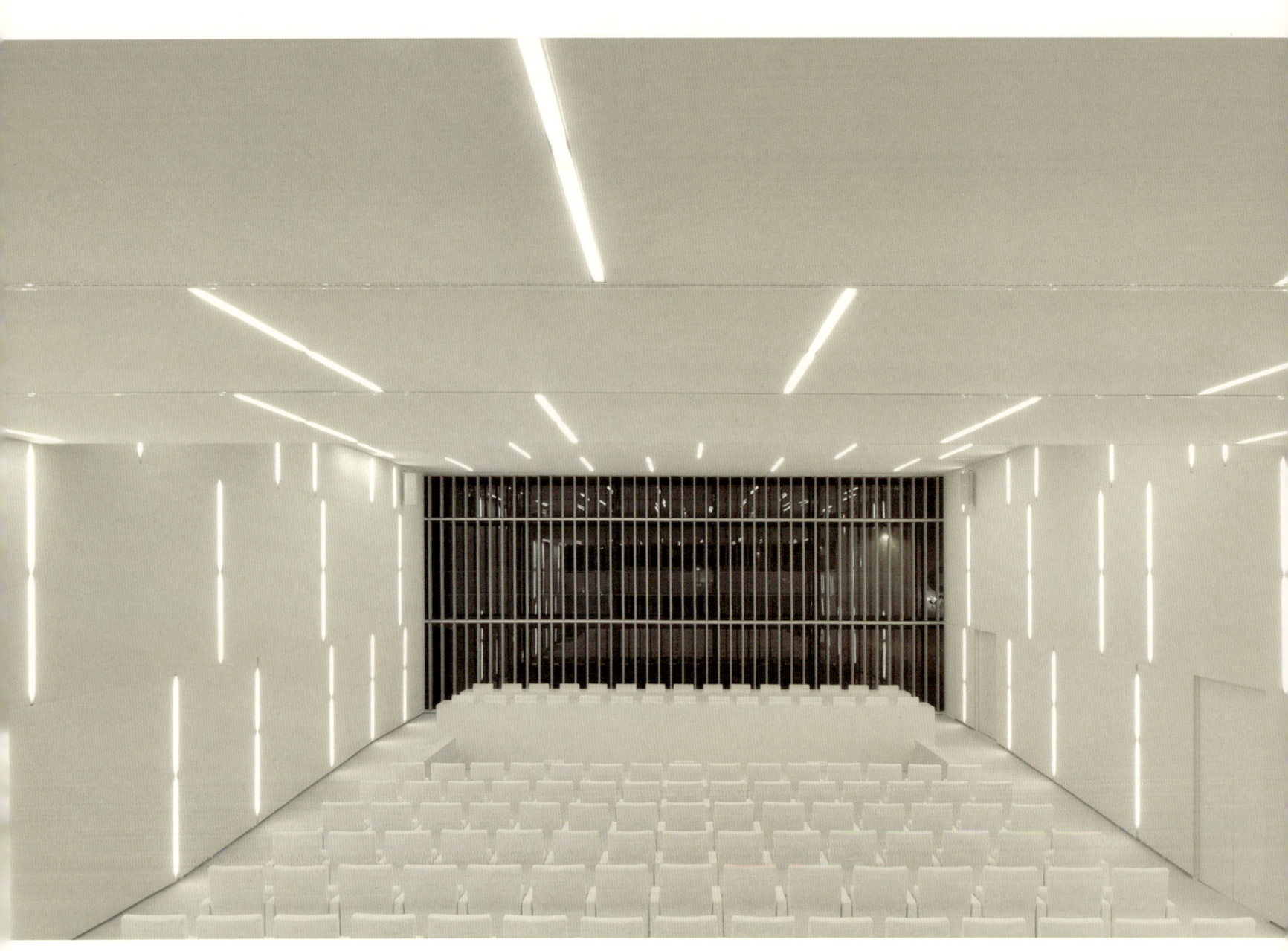

The architecture office heri&salli designed the square in front of the Museum Quarter in Vienna. The result is a constructed sequence of standstill, a moment of physical tranquility. The open space of the Museum Quarter is already considered to be a place in which to hang out and relax, and now the architects have created a prototype of urban space in this area – the Flederhaus, which is also equipped with hammocks. The obviously abstract shape of the house diverges from more traditional ideas of house construction and, because of its different use and the spatial opening, becomes an enlarged public space.

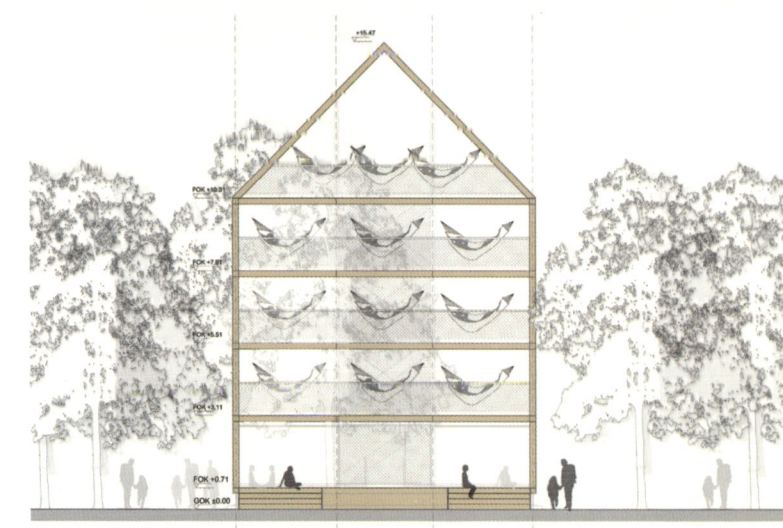

FLEDERHAUS

Two walls, a roof, balconies and hammocks. What else do you need for a quiet afternoon of sunbathing in an urban atmosphere? Hang out.

Architects | heri&salli
Project address | Museumsplatz 1, 1070 Vienna, Austria
Gross floor area | 270 m²
Main materials | wood
Completion | 2011

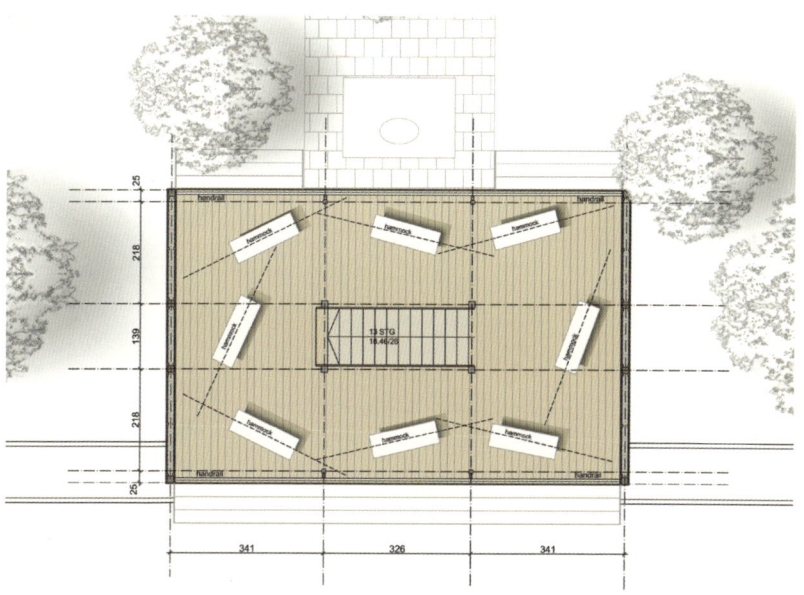

TOR149

Architecture rethought. An avant-garde sculpture in the heart of Berlin.

Architects | GRAFT - Gesellschaft von Architekten mbH
Project address | Torstraße 149, 10119 Berlin, Germany
Gross floor area | 2,461 m²
Main materials | aluminum
Completion | 2013

This innovative and elegant residential house is located in the center of Berlin. An avant-garde and sculptural construction, the building is characterized by its faceted aluminum façade, the unusual lobby and the functional split-level living space. The split-level construction provides the residents with a generously proportioned living area. The interior design is minimalistic, simple and makes the interior space appear larger than it is. For the façade, simple materials and proportions are combined to create the maximum effect with minimal elements. The simplicity of the interior and exterior design gives the building a dignified elegance.

Terrace
Balcony
Bedroom
Media Room
Split 1.1
Split 1.2
Living / Dining Room
Bedroom
Media Room
Split 1.1
Split 1.2
Living / Dining Room
Master
Bedroom
Dressing Room
Split 1.3
Split 1.2
Living / Dining Room

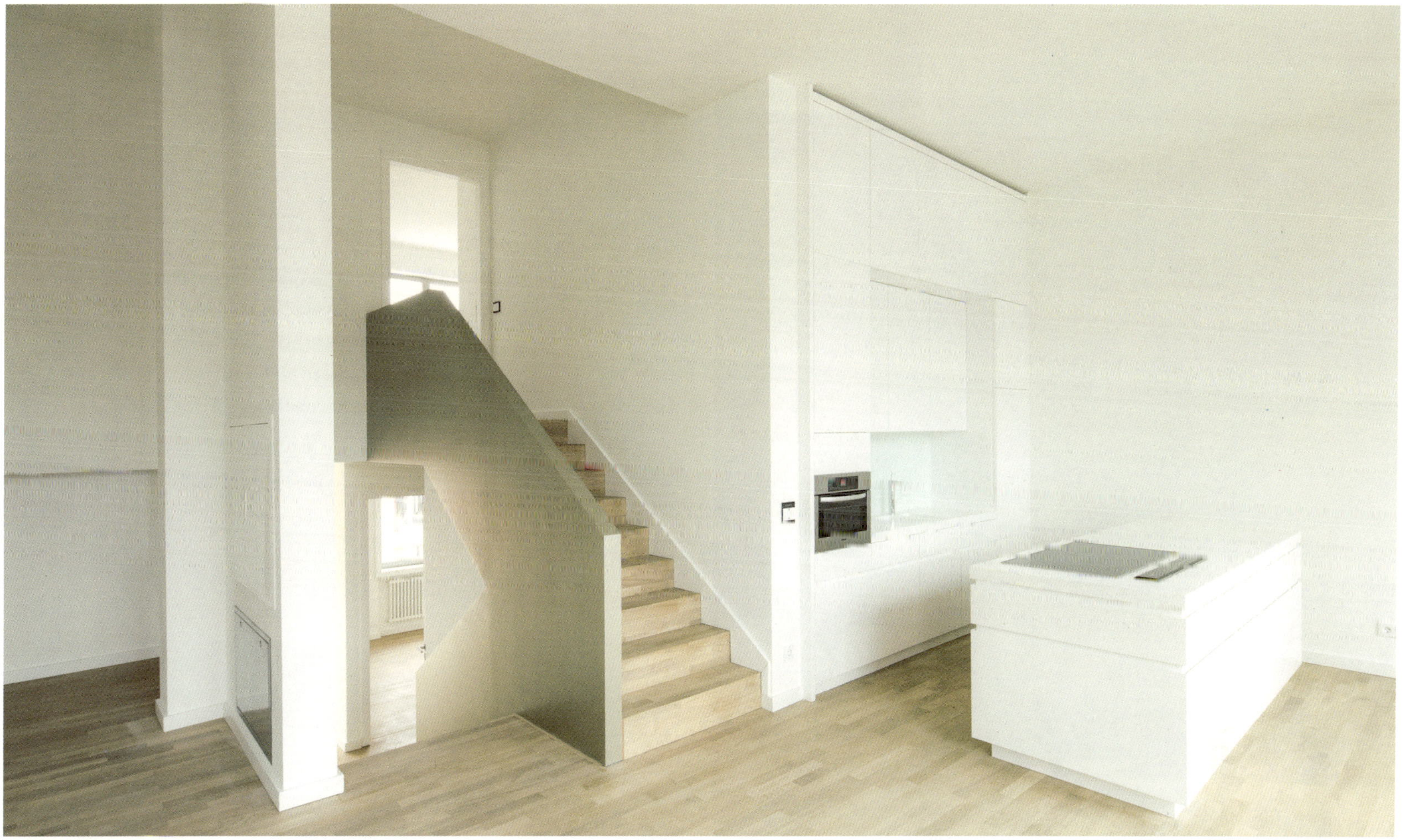

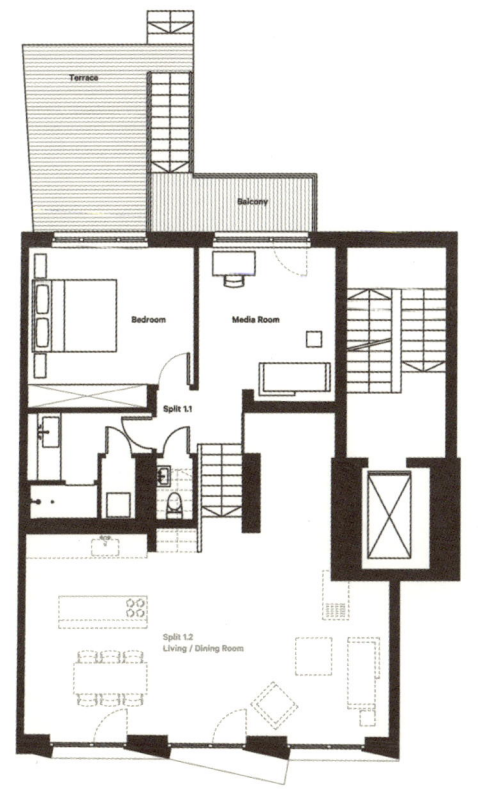

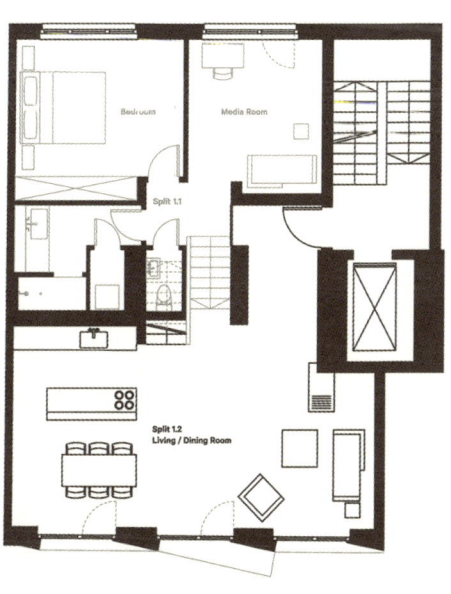

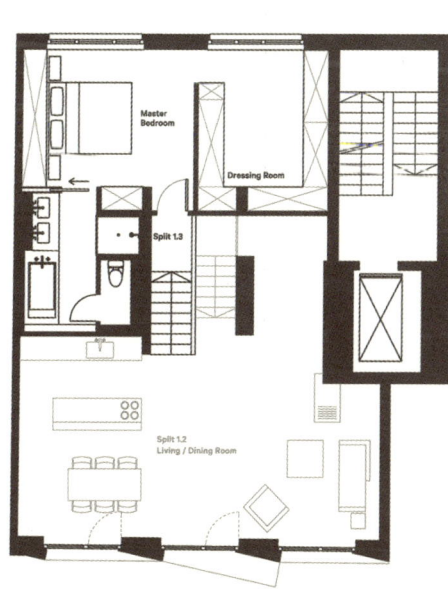

Architects | Mark Merer
Project address | 23 Quaperlake Street, Bruton, BA10 0HF, United Kingdom
Gross floor area | 211 m²
Main materials | corten Steel, burnt red cedar
Completion | 2013

Ferrum House has been built using structurally insulated panels with burnt timber cladding on the ground floor and corten steel cladding on the first and second floors. The building sits alongside an old bacon factory which has been converted into flats. Corten steel was chosen to echo the industrial heritage of the site and sits comfortably near the stone wall of the old factory on the east boundary. The steel cube is set back from the road and perches on top of the burnt cedar clad ground floor. The top two floors of the cube give the illusion of being perched on the timber base while the northern end projects out over the front entrance.

FERRUM HOUSE

Architectural anachronism: Rough corten steel panels next to stone houses – this unexpected mix creates a stunning effect.

229

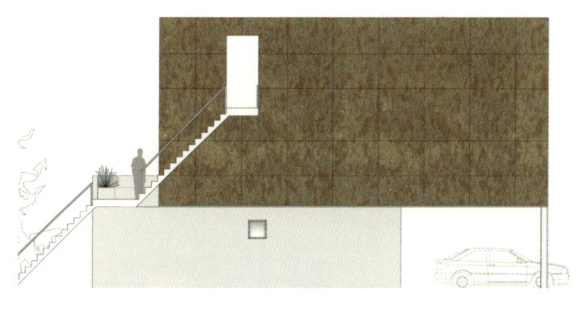

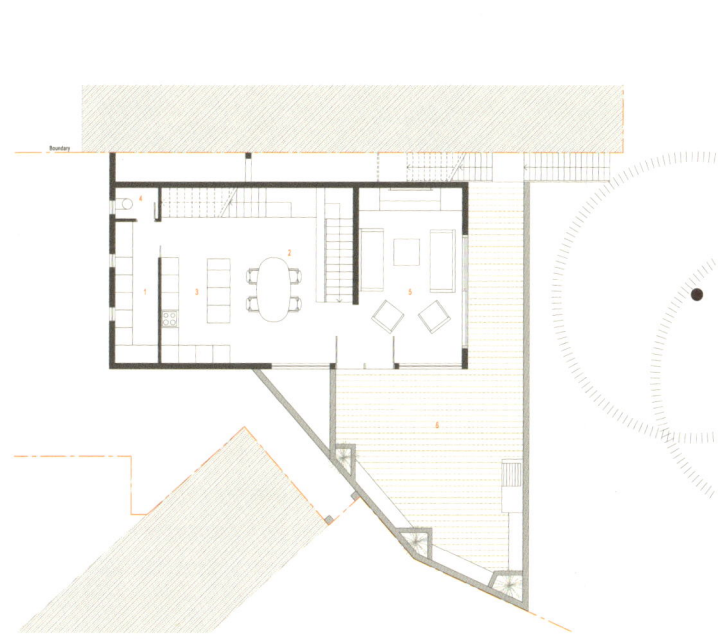

ATRESADOS

Apparently an unlikely couple: But the grey concrete slabs and the round colored tiles form a harmonious unit.

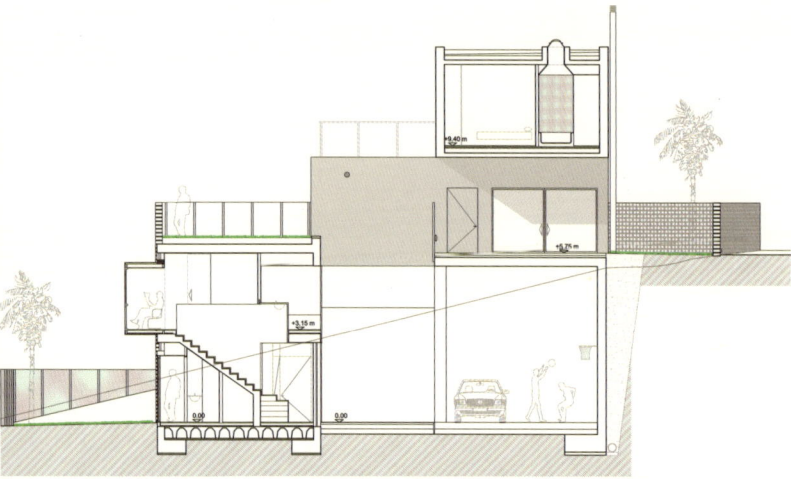

Architects | Javier Peña Galiano
Project address | Avenida Región de Murcia, P-31-13 and P.31-14, 30579 Torreagüera, Spain
Gross floor area | 304 m²
Main materials | ceramics, glazed ceramic, concrete
Completion | 2008

The design of these two houses was based on the idea of redistributing two plots. The two houses are situated at a height that makes the most of the width of the new plot. The lower façade is composed of two distinct elements; the first is the 'wine rack' section, which comprises the principle module of the two houses. The second, is the series of circular tiles of distinct colors made by a local craftsman. These are distributed according to a fading pattern that places the color green in the lower zone, like a continuation of the garden, fading to blue in the upper creating a harmony between the colors of the sky and the gaps in the lattice. Both houses exploit regulation to their own advantage, for example the type of roofs that can be used, which allowed for the construction of green terraces that can be used by each of the houses.

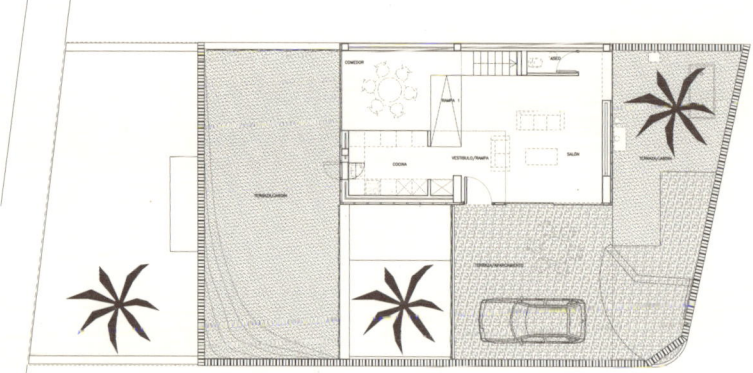

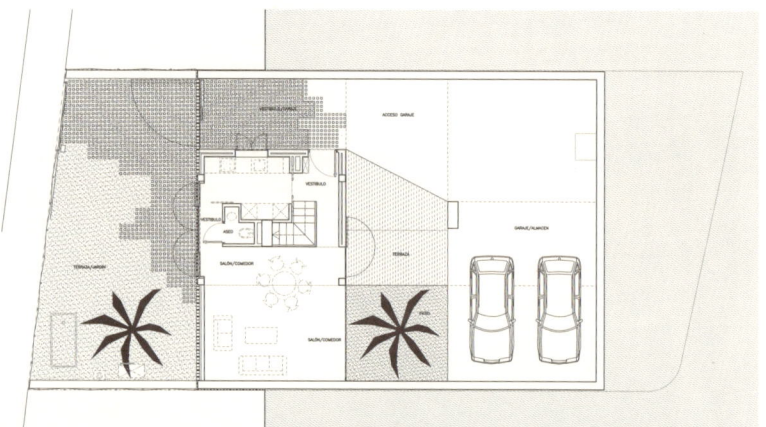

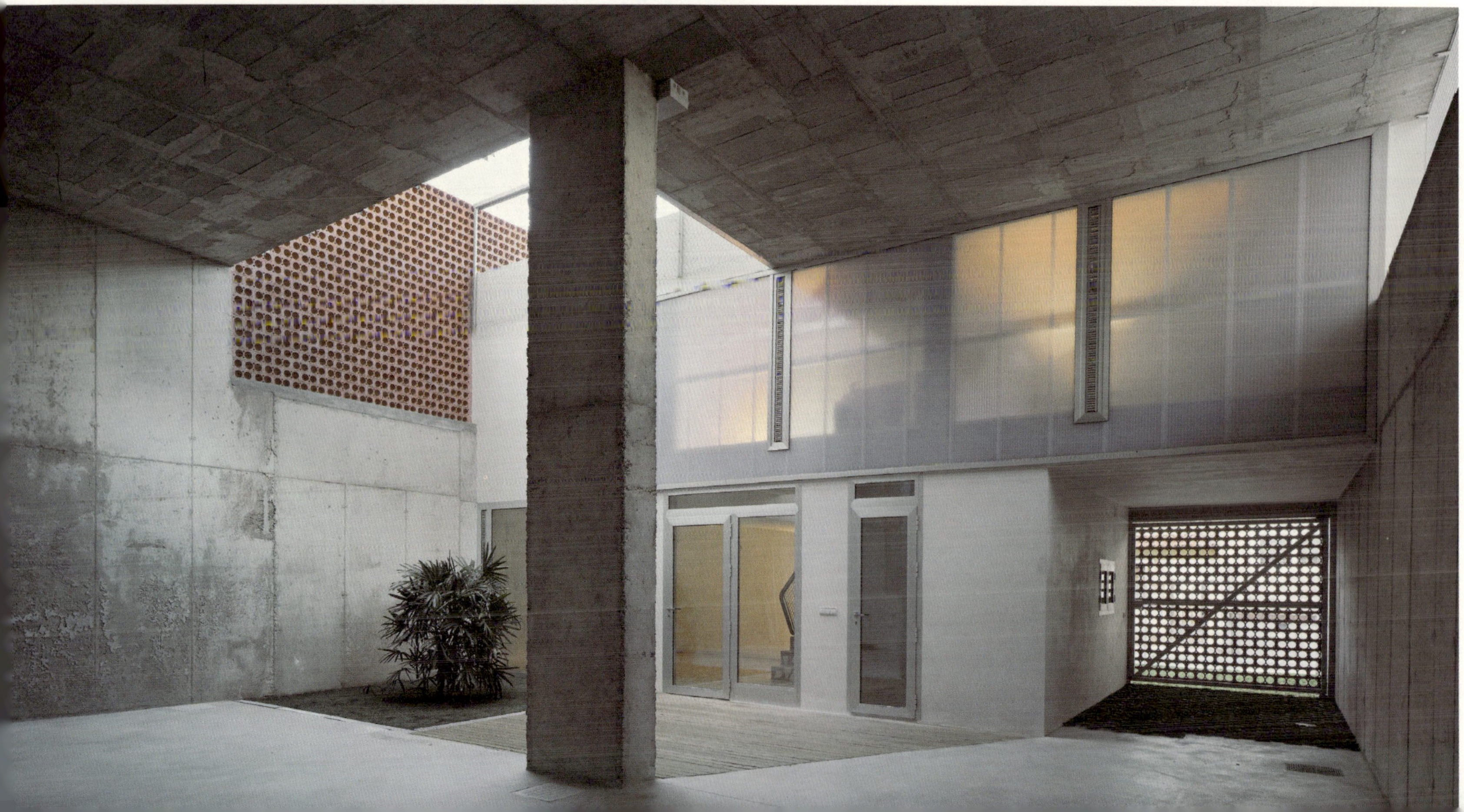

Located in Canton Zurich, the Rhine Falls visitor center defines the entry to Laufen castle and the pathway leading to Europe's largest waterfall. The program required integrating a souvenir shop, bistro, public toilet facilities and a multipurpose hall into an existing staff house. The difficult task of transforming the nondescript house into a public building was achieved by extending the pitched roof and developing a new skin that wraps the entire structure. The new façade, made of weatherproof steel plates, forms a suit of armor that unifies the building into a primary form. On the ground level, folded canopies reveal a second layer with entries, vitrines and a ticket counter. The perforated steel elements on the upper level filter sunlight into the multipurpose hall.

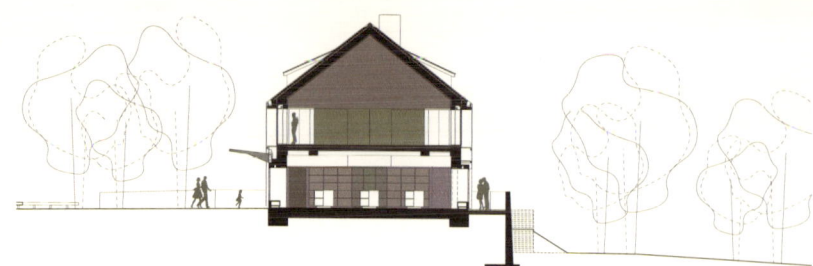

RHINE FALLS VISITOR CENTER

Simple but efficient: An armor-like veil unifies old
and new into a primary form.

Architects | Leuppi & Schafroth Architekten
Project address | Schloss Laufen, 8248 Laufen-Uhwiesen, Switzerland
Original building | Rene Pulver Architekt, 1958
Gross floor area | 1,490 m²
Main materials | weatherproof steel
Completion | 2010

237

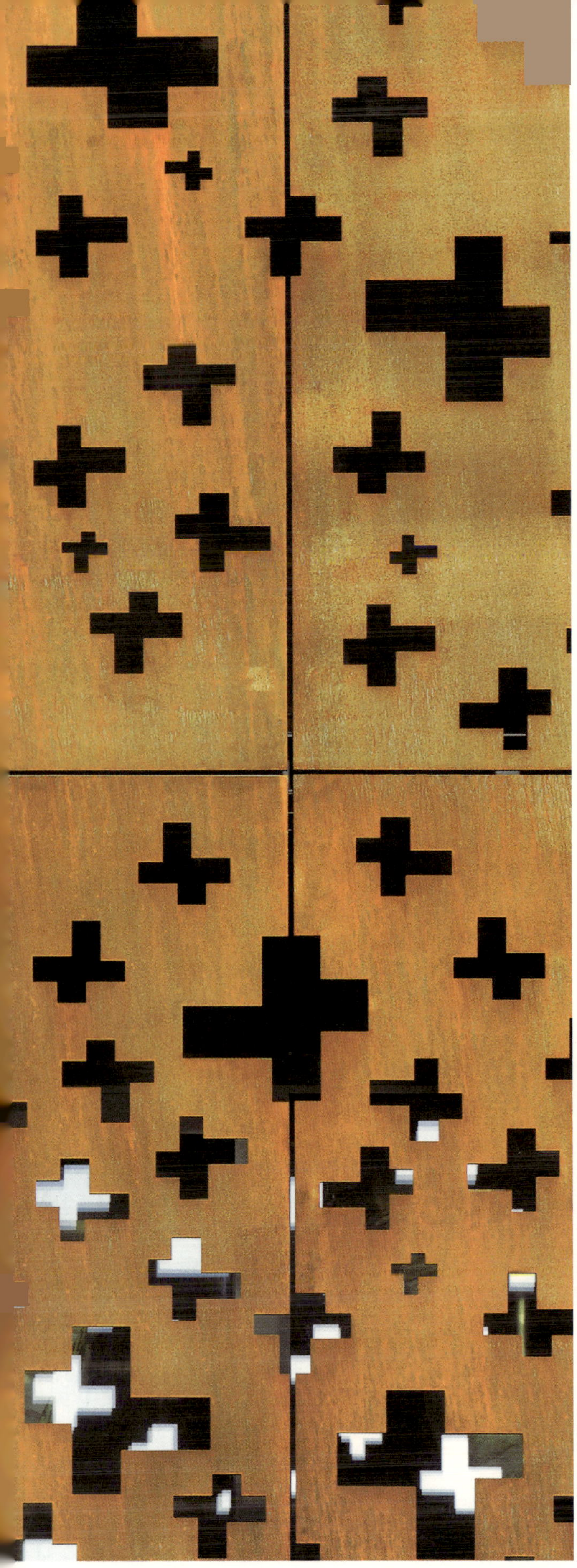

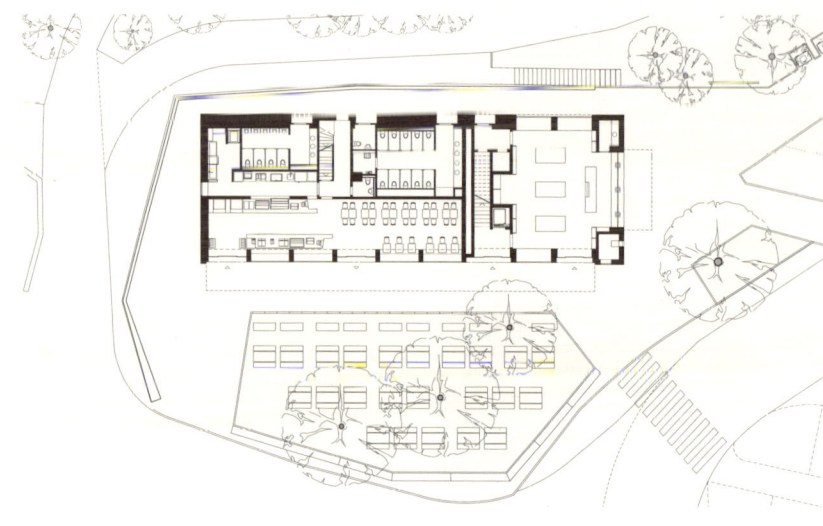

239

ALTER HOF LORENZISTOCK

A barcode on a roof? No. A modern interpretation of the red roofed buildings of Munich's historical Old Town.

Architects | Peter Kulka Architektur
Project address | Diener Straße 12, 80331 Munich, Germany
Gross floor area | 10,240 m²
Main materials | metal, glass
Completion | 2008

The architectural history of the Alter Hof can be traced back to the 13th century. A heterogeneous ensemble of five buildings has been developed over time. In one of these five components, the Lorenzistock on Marienhof, historical vaulted ceilings combine with creative preservation and restoration work carried out by Rudolf Esterer after the Second World War. The addition of an extra level and extension work were limited by the historical nature of the building, but can be seen as a new façade level and in the design of the roof. The new exterior skin of metal and glass elements has been covered with irregular oxide red print. The abstract shining volume corresponds with or contrasts the adjacent red roofs of the historical buildings, depending on the time of day and light. A new gallery level has been added under the new roof, serving as a 'Sky Lounge' and offering stunning views across Munich.

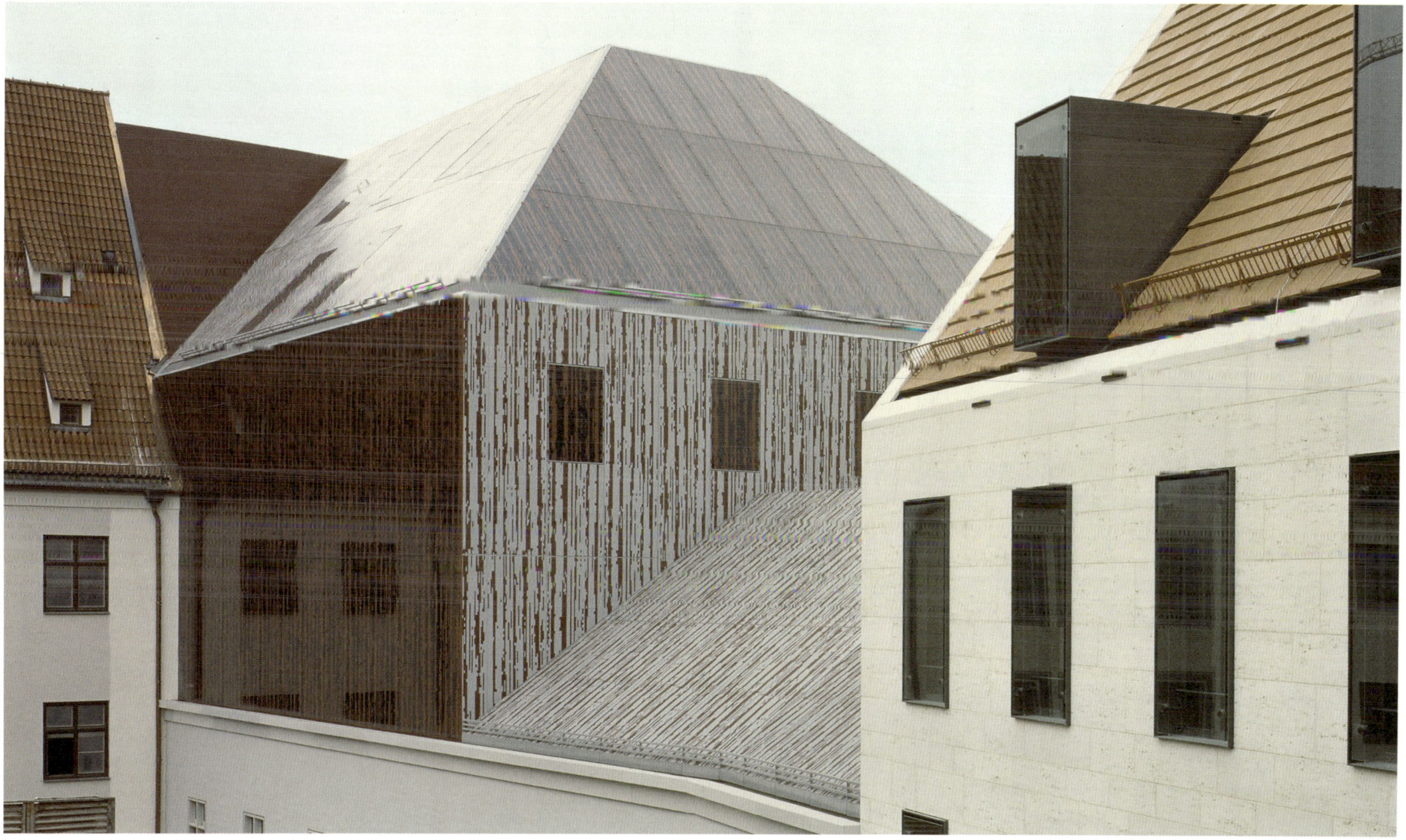

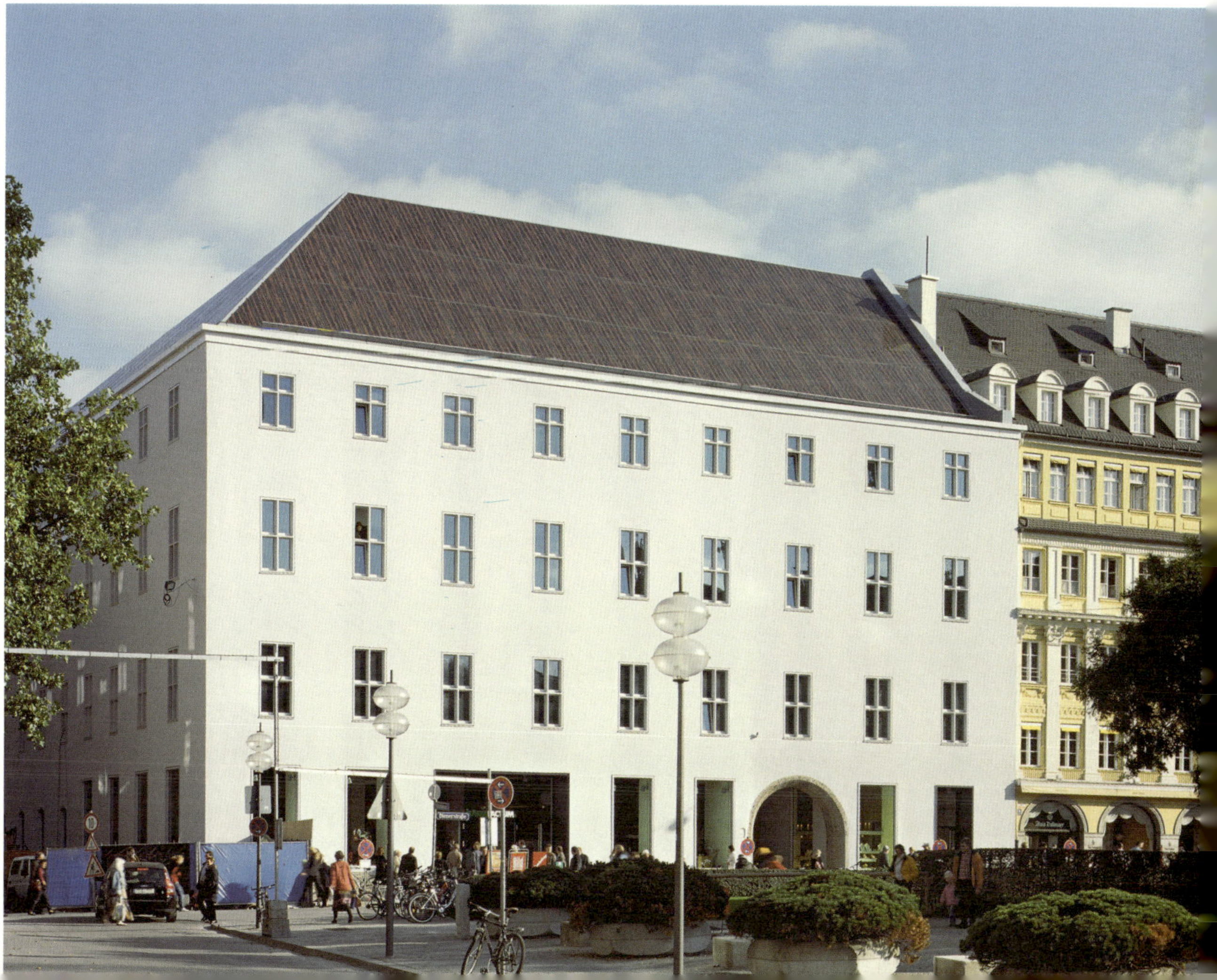

This is a project to remodel the government-owned historical landmark "Customhouse in the Sea" (Dogana di Mare) into a modern art museum. The competition was held in Venice and finally became a battle between the two teams of Zaha Hadid + Guggenheim Foundation and Tadao Ando + Pinault Foundation (Palazzo Grassi). The building comprises a triangular plan with a perimeter that follows the shape of the coastline, with exterior walls of the same red brick. The architects were requested to structurally reinforce this dilapidated building, and having incorporated defenses against rising water levels, to renovate it as a museum for displaying contemporary art. The architects exposed the bricks walls and the wooden roof trusses, in order to further emphasize the charm of the spaces. In a city full of historical charm, this museum will give visitors the chance to enjoy a special and unique experience.

244

PUNTA DELLA DOGANA
CONTEMPORARY ART CENTER

Take what you get. The triangular form of Venice's
new gallery follows the shape of the coastline.
Simple, rational, beautiful.

Architects | Tadao Andó Architect & Associates
Project address | Dorsoduro 2, 30123, Venice, Italy
Gross floor area | 4,585 m²
Main materials | wood, concrete, brick
Completion | 2009

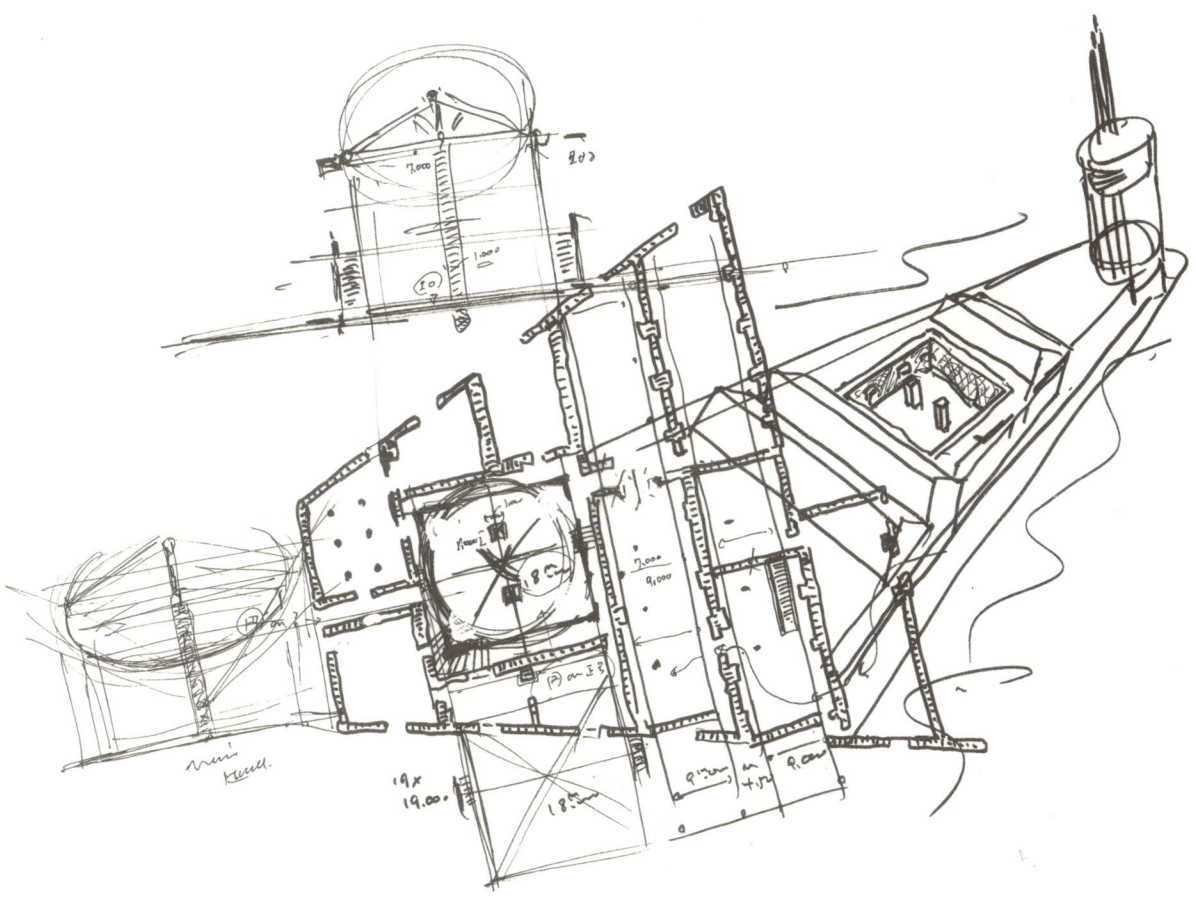

246

TOWNHOUSE OBERWALL

Successful operation. Once a half-finished townhouse, now the home of a fashion designer and his label.

This project involved the transformation of a half-finished townhouse into a flagship store for a fashion label and a second home for the designers. The building structures was dismantled and redesigned. The new design makes the most of the typical vertical orientation of a townhouse. The façade concept is radically minimalist in style. The façade gives the house its unique character, creating an unmistakable face for the company. The white building envelope comprises highly polished lacquered aluminum panels. A fully glazed sliding door forms the entrance to the store; this is six-and-a-half meters tall and just as tall as the building is wide. The seven-story building houses two duplexes. Working and living environments are united under one roof. The reduced color pallet focuses on white, natural white, and concrete gray, thus emphasizing the effect of natural light.

Architects | apool/Dominik Franz, Jesper Reinholt
Project address | Oberwallstraße 16, 10117 Berlin, Germany
Gross floor area | 540 m²
Main materials | aluminum, glass, concrete
Completion | 2012

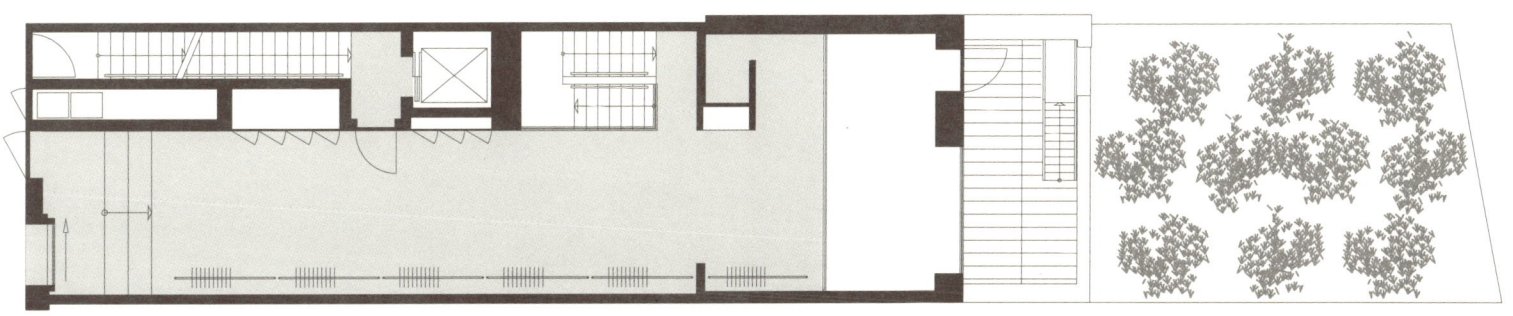

The Velvet State arose as an ambition to combine performance and architecture to create one project at the Roskilde Festival 2013. The core of the project emerged via an ongoing dialogue between the performers and the architects, adopting and merging the two disciplines into one. Simon Hjermind Jensen from Shjworks (DK) designed the building, while the performance part was developed in a dialogue between Fiction Pimps (DK) and Collective Unconscious (UK), directed by Inga Gerner Nielsen. The physical structure comprises seven parts: The Ring, The Stage, The Ridge, The Reactor, The Barn, The Dressing Room and The Courtyard. All parts were built in shells of plywood. The plywood shells acted both as façade and as support for the structure. The thick plywood was placed at the bottom and the thin at the top. Each plywood shell was bent into a singular curve and all together these curves created the structural support for the whole project.

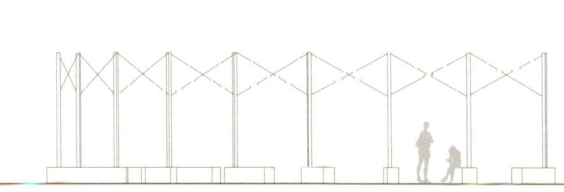

THE VELVET STATE

Architecture meets performance: This colony of little plywood shells forms an inspiring and secure circle for the artists.

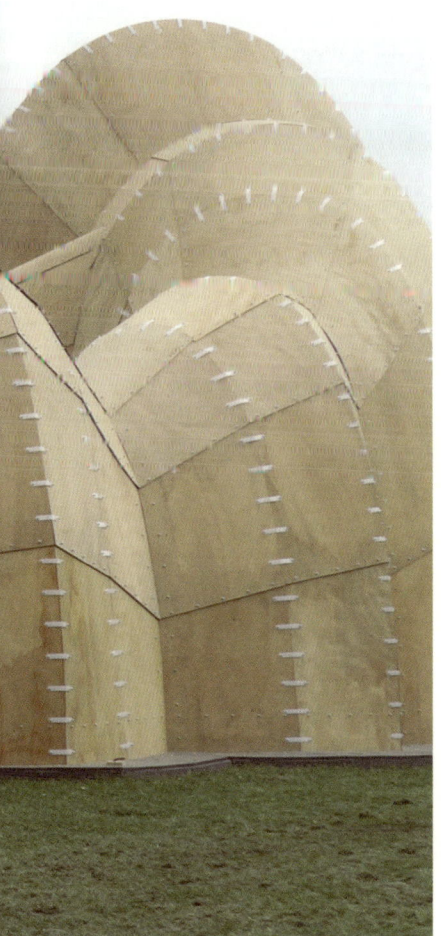

Architects | Shjworks
Project address | Darupvej 19, 4000 Roskilde County, Denmark
Gross floor area | 177 m²
Main materials | wood
Completion | 2013

253

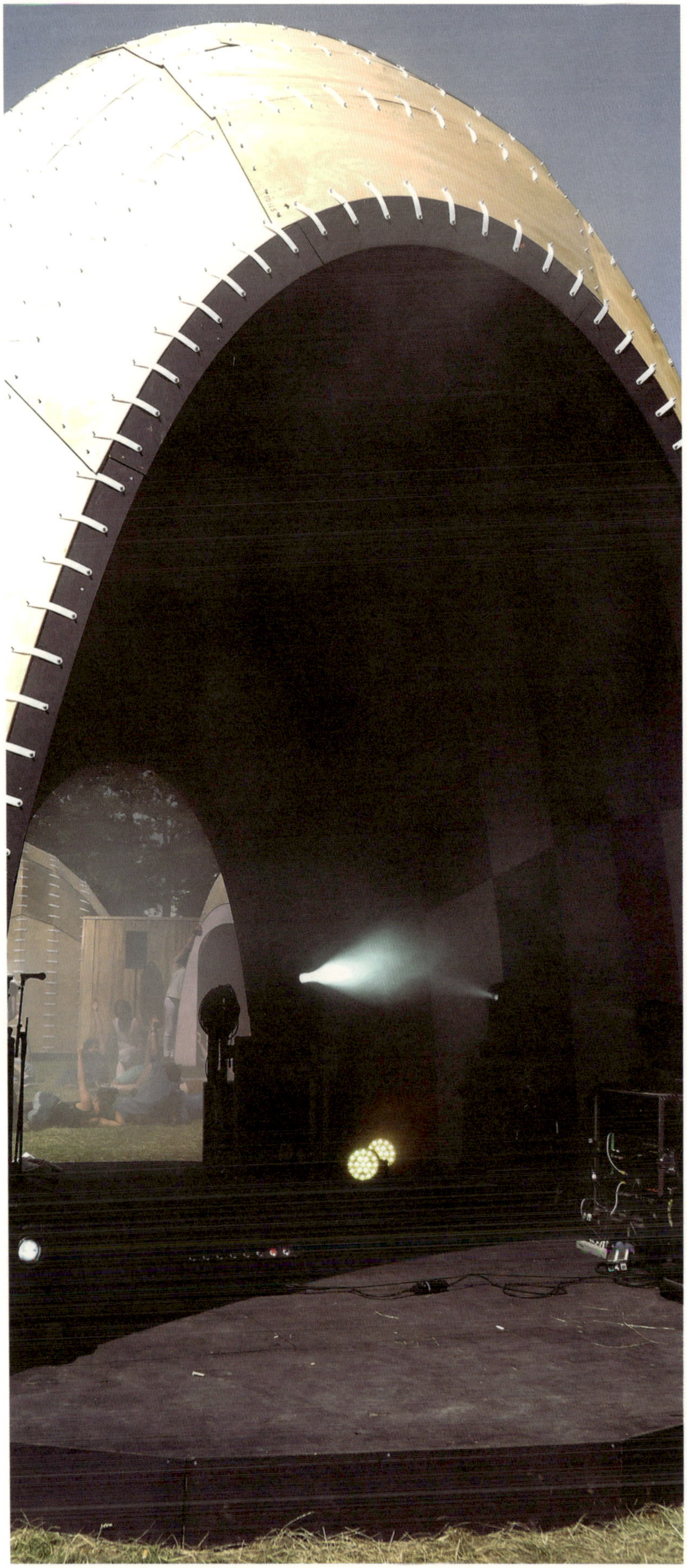
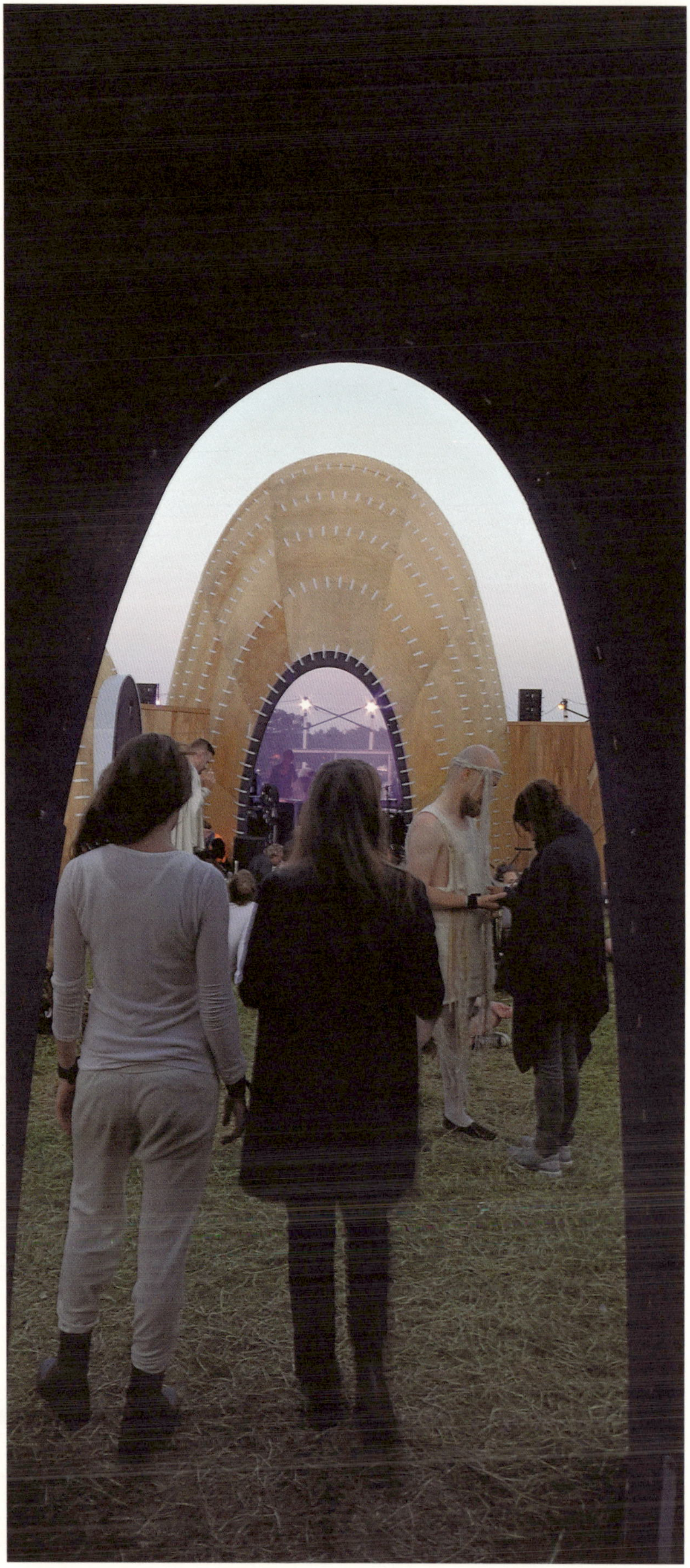

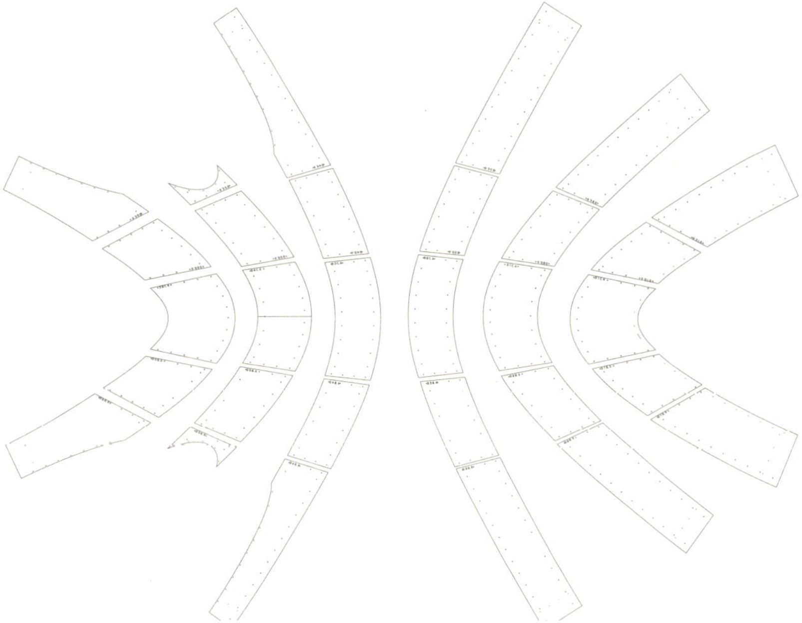

Bridge Studio is one of the Fogo Island Art Corporation Art Studios. The simple architectural style compliments the natural surroundings: the first sight as one approaches the studio is of a solar panel, which makes the most of the area's limited sunshine. From the side, the studio appears closed and hovers above the landscape raised on four piers. The glazed open entry contrasts the closed side elevation. The studio slopes upwards from the entry, towards a large glass window at the other end. A desk is located beneath the window – the perfect place to sit and work.

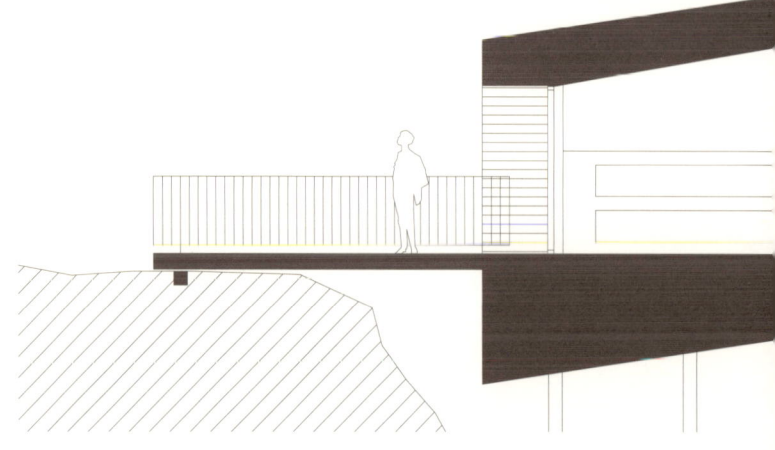

BRIDGE STUDIO

Is there any better source of inspiration than a beautiful landscape? You can call yourself lucky if your desk is out there in the wilderness.

Architects | Saunders Architecture
Project address | Fogo Island, Newfoundland, Canada
Gross floor area | 130 m²
Main materials | woo
Completion | 2011

259

261

In the heart of a 150-acre redwood forest, Smith|Allen has created Echoviren, a site re-sponsive, 3D printed architectural installation Echoviren. The project merges architec-ture, art and technology to explore the dialectic between man, machine and nature. Echoviren is a simple shelter, a hermitage, a place of temporary rest and contempla-tion of the forest. Walking around and within the structure, the viewer is immediately consumed by the juxtaposition, as well as uncanny similarity, of natural and unnatural. Made of over 500 unique individually printed parts, the structure is assembled though a paneled snap fit connection, merging individual components into a monolithic ag-gregation. The space will decompose naturally back into the forest in 30 to 50 years. Echoviren exposes an ecosystem of dynamic natural and unnatural interventions: the interplay of man and nature moderated by technology over the centuries.

ECHOVIREN PAVILION

Man. Machine. Nature. Explore the uncanny
similarity between natural and unnatural

Architects | Smith|Allen
Project address | 387 Project, Highway 1 Gualala, CA, USA
Gross floor area | 4 m²
Main materials | PLA 3D printed bioplastic
Completion | 2013

265

2by4-architects have designed this unique recreational house, located on an island in the Dutch lake Loosdrechtse Plas. The house deliberately develops a dialogue with the surrounding nature. One of the glass façades can be completely opened so that the wooden outdoor terrace becomes part of the interior. The dark timber façade can also be opened, thus further blurring the boundaries between inside and outside. By opening this part of the façade the wooden floor of the living area is now directly connected to the water. Although the size of the house is limited it still contains all the functions that are needed for comfort, all integrated into a double wall. The wall can be modified so that the spatial configuration changes, resulting into different atmospheres. The fireplace hangs from the ceiling and can be rotated towards the outdoor terrace for those cozy summer evenings.

THE ISLAND HOUSE

Open Sesame! You were in the living room and as if
by magic, you find yourself just beside the water.

Architects | 2by4-architects
Project address | Loosdrechtse Plas, Breukelen, The Netherlands
Gross floor area | 21 m²
Main materials | glass, wood, steel frames, wooden deck, epoxy floor
Completion | 2012

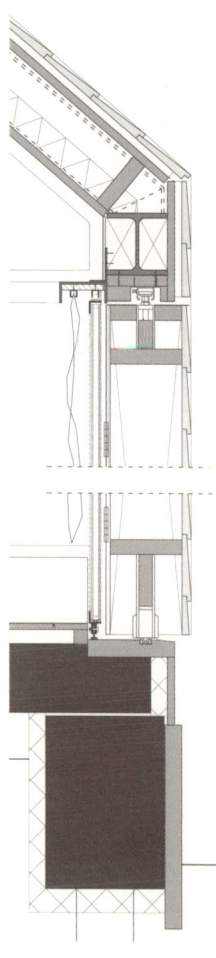

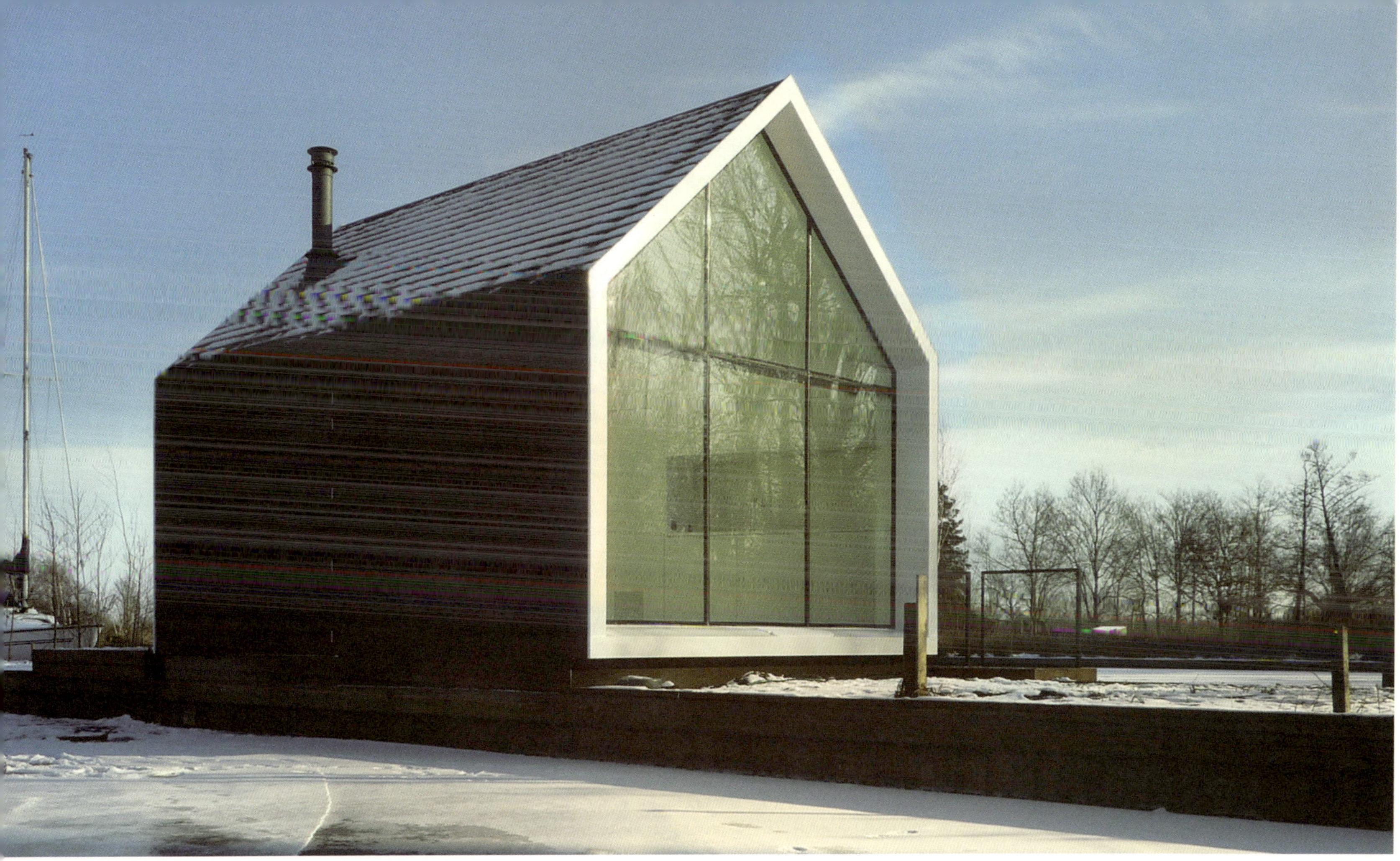

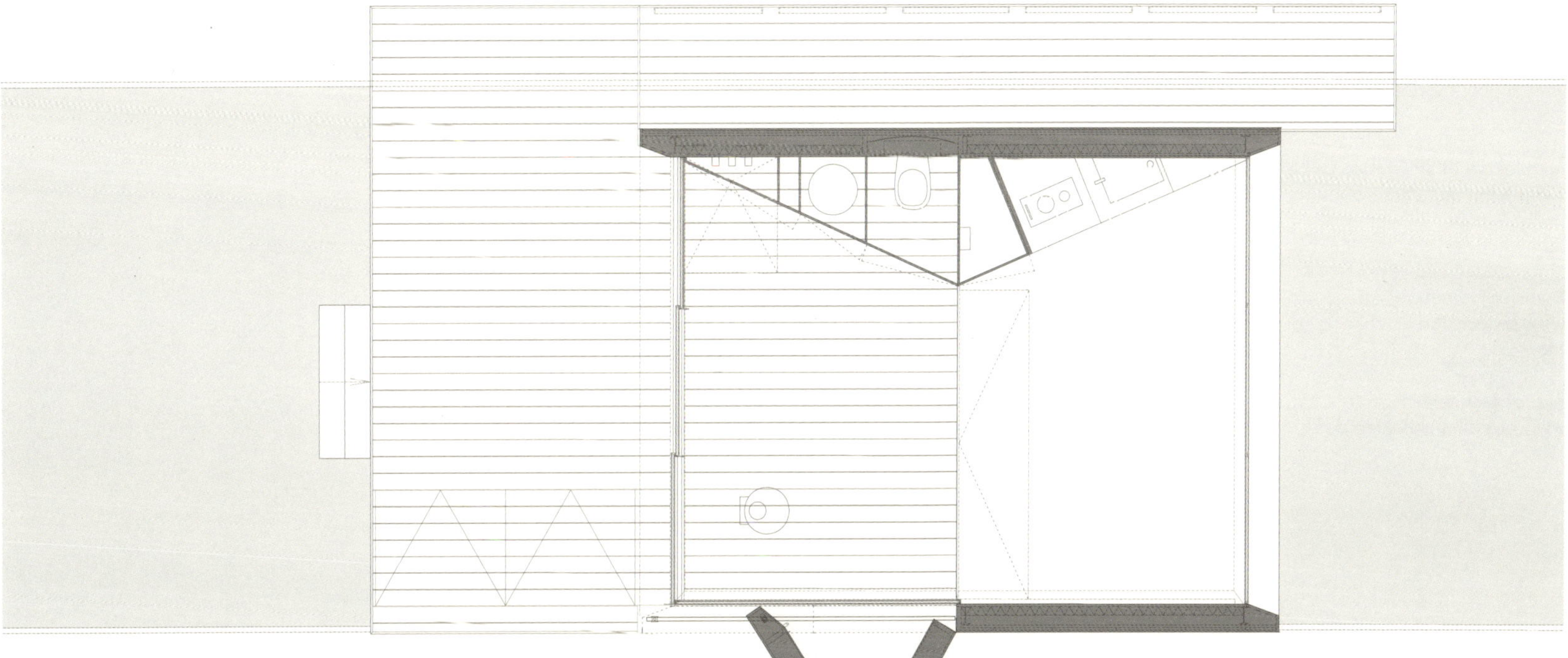

INDEX

PICTURE CREDITS

All other pictures were made available by the architects.

Cover front: Marc Cramer, Montreal
Cover back: Bent René Synnevåg

IMPRINT

The Deutsche Nationalbibliothek lists this publication in the Deutsche Nationalbibliografie; detailed bibliographic data are available in the Internet at http://dnb.dnb.de

ISBN 978-3-03768-164-0
© 2014 by Braun Publishing AG
www.braun-publishing.ch

1st edition 2014

Editor: Chris van Uffelen
Editorial staff and layout: Lisa Rogers
Graphic concept: Michaela Prinz, Berlin
Reproduction: Bild1Druck GmbH, Berlin